CLIMBERS' GUIDE
TO GLENCOE AND ARDGOUR

CLIMBERS' GUIDE TO

GLENCOE AND ARDGOUR

VOLUME 1

BUACHAILLE ETIVE MOR

BY

L. S. LOVAT

Published by

W. & R. CHAMBERS LTD, EDINBURGH

FOR

THE SCOTTISH MOUNTAINEERING TRUST

1967

First Edition ... 1949
Reprinted 1967

PRINTED IN GREAT BRITAIN BY
ROBERT CUNNINGHAM AND SONS LTD, ALVA

CONTENTS

MAPS AND DIAGRAMS

INTRODUCTION

In the opening sentence of his introduction to the first edition in 1949 of the Glencoe and Ardgour Guide, W. H. Murray wrote—"The supreme delight of rock-climbing is that of exploration." The truth of this is once again demonstrated, for this second edition comprises two volumes, first, the Buachaille Etive Mor and, second, the rest of Glencoe, Trilleachan Slabs and Ardgour. The number of routes has been approximately doubled since 1949.

I have adhered, to a great extent, to the style of description of routes adopted by W. H. Murray and to the underlying principle of encouraging judgment by deliberate compromise between the extremes of vagueness and detail. This sounds rather solemn, not to say grim. Yet I hope that those using this Guide will have as much fun as I had preparing it.

The rock-climbs are all graded for vibrams. This has caused a good deal of amendment of grades. In this and in the ultimate resolution of graded lists, which have now been inserted, I shall be responsible for any errors, which will be, I hope, on the side of over-grading.

In describing routes and particularly their starts, I have indulged in much repetition so as to avoid, as far as possible, the irritation of cross-references to starts and features of other routes. It is the lesser of two evils. The descriptions of recent winter ascents are sometimes scanty. I have preferred the description, in some instances, of conditions experienced by the first party, to generalisation, which is often more misleading. Readers will bear in mind that in these instances, grades and times may mean even less than they normally do.

I wish to thank the following for the indispensable assistance which they gave me: W. H. Murray, J. R. Marshall and R. G. Inglis (Guide-books General Editor), for their revisal of the manuscripts and good advice; J. R. Marshall and W. C. Harrison for diagrams; Mrs J. C. Donaldson; various members of the S.M.C., J.M.C.S. and Creagh Dhu M.C. for much information and advice and for opinions on the draft graded lists; and, perhaps above all, my many friends who climbed the routes with me. In doing so, it is right to point out that, in preparing the second edition, I am simply continuing the work of my predecessor and his helpers, to whom we all remain indebted.

NOTES ON THE USE OF THE GUIDE

(a) *Rock-climbs*

The following terms have been used:

> Easy
> Moderate
> Difficult
> Very Difficult
> Severe
> Very Severe

These gradings are given for vibrams and dry conditions. A list in order of difficulty has been drawn up for each of four regions, the Buachaille Etive Mor, the rest of Glencoe, the Trilleachan (Loch Etive) Slabs and Ardgour. The reliability of such lists is, of course, limited.

(b) *Winter routes*

The rock-climbing terms have been used. But the technique of snow and ice climbing is sufficiently removed from that of rock-climbing and the difficulties themselves are usually so different in nature, that no parallel should be drawn, objectively or subjectively. Variability of conditions is such that precision of grading is even more difficult than for rock-climbs and graded lists have not been attempted. Routes have not been included unless properly snow-bound or ice-bound.

Left and Right Directions

"Left" and "right" refer only to a climber facing upwards.

ROPE LENGTHS

Between two climbers, 120 feet is the recommended length.

HEIGHTS

The heights of climbs have been estimated by eye and by measured rope-lengths. Many estimates have been reached by the addition of pitch-estimates, particularly on walls and slabs. There will be plenty of errors. But the climber is more concerned with the run-out of rope than with vertical height. Only the Chasm and Clachaig Gully heights have been determined by theodolite from measured base lines.

MAPS

The following maps are recommended: One-inch Ordnance Survey, Sheet No. 47, "Glen Coe", for Glencoe; and One-inch Ordnance Survey, Sheet No. 46, "Loch Linnhe", for Ardgour.

ACCOMMODATION

There is plenty of accommodation in the Glencoe region. Good camping ground is available all about the area. At the east end of Glencoe will be found Lagan-garbh Cottage (S.M.C.), Blackrock Cottage (Ladies' Scottish Climbing Club) and Kingshouse Hotel; at the west end, the S.Y.H.A. Hostel at Clachaig and Clachaig Hotel. There are other places of accommodation further west at Glencoe Village and Ballachulish.

KEY TO MAP ON PAGE 2

1 Glen Etive	6 Gearr Aonach
2 Buachaille Etive Mor	7 Stob Coire nan Lochan
3 Lairig Gartain	8 Aonach Dubh
4 Buachaille Etive Beag	9 Glencoe
5 Beinn Fhada	10 Sgor nam Fiannaidh

INDEX TO THE ROUTES

The column headed "No." refers to the page number of the diagram on which the climb appears; "N.C." indicates that the climb has not been graded.

THE BUACHAILLE ETIVE MOR

THE NORTH-EAST FACE

THE BUACHAILLE ETIVE MOR

THE Buachaille Etive Mor lies in the angle between Glencoe and Glen Etive. The mountain is a long ridge with four tops. The summit is the north top, Stob Dearg (3345 feet), popularly known as "The Buachaille". The best rock-climbing in Glencoe is to be had on its northerly and easterly faces, which converge gracefully above the Moor of Rannoch. An excellent viewpoint is approximately one mile west of the Glencoe-Glen Etive crossroads.

The Buachaille is one of the most elegant mountains in Britain. It provides first-class summer and winter climbing of all grades of difficulty. The rock is a coarse and reliable rhyolite. The routes are described from north-west to south-east under three main headings: the North Face, the North-East Face, and the South-East Face.

EASY DESCENTS. Easy routes of descent, free from rock, may be found by going from the summit 300 yards west-south-west (magnetic) along the level summit ridge, then 300 yards due west to a col at 2900 feet. Thence either turn north down Coire na Tulaich to Lagangarbh Cottage in Glencoe (3 miles west of Kingshouse Inn), or else turn south down Coire Cloiche Finne to Glen Etive (2½ miles south of the Glencoe road). From the summit, these are the most convenient routes of descent in winter, particularly for those who do not know the mountain well.

In summer, the most commonly used routes of descent from the summit are Curved Ridge and North Buttress (apart from the easy descents already described). They should not be used in winter. Great Gully is an inferior

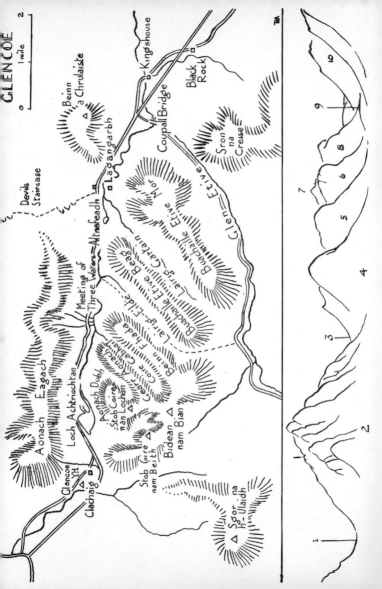

route of descent in summer and a dangerous or slow one in winter. To reach Curved Ridge from the summit descend due east magnetic to Crowberry Tower Gap, skirt the Tower by an easy gully on its right, and go left at the base to the top of Curved Ridge.

COIRE NA TULAICH

The entrance to this great north-western corrie of Buachaille is directly above Lagangarbh. The corrie is flanked on the east by Stob Dearg and lower, on the west, by Stob Coire nan Tuileachan.

On the lowest slopes of Stob Coire nan Tuileachan west of the corrie is a crag named Creag a' Bhancair. It presents to the glen a 300-foot face, on which pleasant, steep climbing has been found near the west edge. The exceptionally steep, central part has been climbed by the following route:

CARNIVORE   655 feet   VERY SEVERE

J. Cunningham and M. Noon. 9th August 1958.

This route begins near the north-east corner of the west face, to the right of The Chimney described below. It follows an obvious and very steep line diagonally rightwards across the wall and its length takes into account some very long traverses.

Start at the left end of the wall at a cairn. The first pitch is 130 feet. Climb up and then rightwards on large holds to a resting-place with a loose block on the left. Continue straight up (avoiding a right traverse to easier ground). After 15 feet make a hand traverse to the right to gain a small ledge. Insert a piton, descend slightly and traverse right for 10 feet to gain a rightward descending fault. Traverse along the fault passing a very small spike

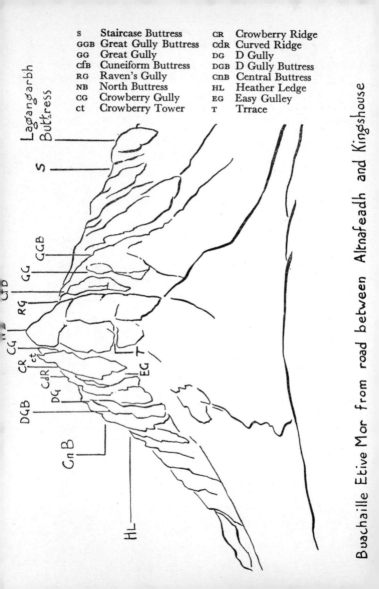

S	Staircase Buttress	CR	Crowberry Ridge
GGB	Great Gully Buttress	cdR	Curved Ridge
GG	Great Gully	DG	D Gully
cfB	Cuneiform Buttress	DGB	D Gully Buttress
RG	Raven's Gully	cnB	Central Buttress
NB	North Buttress	HL	Heather Ledge
CG	Crowberry Gully	EG	Easy Gulley
ct	Crowberry Tower	T	Trrace

Lagangarbh Buttress

Buachaille Etive Mor from road between Altnafeadh and Kingshouse

and then along a shelf reaching a point below a big ledge. Use a piton runner and climb straight up to the ledge where a piton belay can be taken. Walk along the ledge to the far end where a piton belay is taken at 35 feet. Pitch 3 follows the line of a green coloured scoop for 60 feet to a grass ledge on the right and a piton belay. Climb up by grass ledges and by an obvious line of weakness to a crack running rightwards. Climb the crack to a small shelf below a black overhanging recess at 65 feet. Piton belay. Pitch 5 begins with a right traverse across a slab where a piton can be used. Take the line of a horizontal crack beneath overhangs and at 20 feet surmount the overhang, traverse right, using four pitons and gain a sloping ledge. Follow the ledge to a small cave at 70 feet. Piton belay. Continue the traverse (hands under the overhang) with the help of a piton runner at 20 feet and so for a further 30 feet to a large grass ledge and block belay. From the block belay a rising leftward traverse is made with a piton runner at 30 feet. Thereafter move left under a bulge and across to a grass ledge then up the wall above to a small ledge and piton belay. Pitch 8 is 120 feet. Climb straight up to a large grass ledge and piton belay. The final pitch of 50 feet goes by the line of a wall above a small tree to a stance and belay below a large boulder.

THE CHIMNEY OF CREAG A' BHANCAIR

150 feet   VERY DIFFICULT

G. G. Macphee, G. F. Todd, G. C. Williams, I. G. Jack. May 1934.

Near the north-east corner is an obvious chimney. Start at the top of a conspicuous cone of turf. Climb through trees and vegetation to a cave and chimney very near the top. The 15-20-foot crux pitch consists of rock.

Easy Going 455. obvious groove right of dwindle wall – left to ledge rightwards groove/ramp to ledge.

CREAG NA TULAICH

Above and to the east of Creag a' Bhancair, the North-East Ridge of Stob Coire nan Tuileachan rises half-way up into a prominent buttress with short steep flanks. All the rocks about here are suitable for an evening's climbing and four routes are recorded:

DWINDLE WALL   120 feet   VERY SEVERE

R. Smith and A. Frazer. June 1958.

This route follows a zig-zag fault running up rightwards across the steep, west face. Start below the fault at an overhang near the north edge. Finish the route on a delicate slab.

CREST ROUTE   200 feet   MODERATE

G. G. Macphee, G. F. Todd, G. C. Williams, I. G. Jack. May 1934.

Climb the north edge of the west face. Many more difficult variations are possible on excellent rock. (The north edge of the east face also provides a moderate but less interesting route.)

ARROWHEAD GROOVE   150 feet   VERY DIFFICULT

D. H. Haworth and I. McPhail. August 1947.

Start near the south end of the east face at a cairn below a rock arrowhead perched on a platform about 40 feet up the face. To start, either go up about 15 feet rightwards to a platform and, by a short left traverse, gain a shallow groove leading to the arrowhead, or climb the groove direct from below, which is harder. Traverse left above the arrowhead and follow any line to the top of the buttress.

EAST ROUTE   150 feet   MODERATE

D. H. Haworth and G. C. Williams. May 1947.

Start at the south end of the east face a few feet left
of the cairn of Arrowhead Groove. Climb to a square-cut
corner and so by the line of least resistance to the top.

THE NORTH FACE

The North Face of Buachaille includes the cliffs between Coire na Tulaich and North Buttress. These are
in two groups—the Lagangarbh Group and the Great
Gully group. Diagram p. 4.

The Lagangarbh Group comprises three buttresses and
two gullies in the following order from right to left as
seen from a point about half a mile east of Alltnafeidh:
Lagangarbh Buttress, Staircase Buttress, Broad Gully,
Broad Buttress (which is split by a deep groove) and
Narrow Gully. Broad Gully, Broad Buttress and Narrow
Gully are devoid of climbing interest.

The Great Gully Group comprises in the same order:
Great Gully Buttress, Great Gully, Cuneiform Buttress,
Raven's Gully and the West Face of North Buttress.

Access to the Lagangarbh Group is most interestingly
gained by climbing from the lowest rocks below Lagangarbh Buttress. These afford much variation and avoid
a tedious plod. There are many miniature routes in this
Group, which have been included because they provide
excellent sport for an evening or a short day.

LAGANGARBH BUTTRESS

Lagangarbh Buttress is the most westerly buttress on
the North Face. It lies high up on the extreme right of
the Lagangarbh Group and its west face overlooks Coire
na Tulaich. The top section of its north face is split by
the narrow Lagangarbh Chimney.

WEST FACE

PANG   150 feet   VERY SEVERE

J. R. Marshall, G. J. Ritchie and A. H. Hendry. 9th
    June 1956.

Start about 100 feet right of Lagangarbh Chimney
(mentioned above). Cairn. Of two parallel cracks above,
climb first by the right one then by the left to gain a
rock bay. Climb the steep arête on the left to a large
slab ledge and continue to reach a thin crack topped by
a rock spike. Climb the crack.

CREST ROUTE

300 feet to include Slab below Terrace   SEVERE

(200 feet if from Terrace   MODERATE)

J. H. B. Bell and J. R. Wood. A. C. D. Small and Miss
    E. Johnstone. May 1936.

Start at a slab 100 feet below and to the left of Lagangarbh Chimney. Climb the slab (severe) to a terrace
skirting the buttress. Traverse right to Lagangarbh
Chimney and climb the final 200 feet by moderate rock
to the left of it. (After climbing the 100-foot slab, a
better finish is to climb the Left Edge Route described
below.)

LAGANGARBH CHIMNEY   200 feet   DIFFICULT

P. M. Barclay and A. R. Ramsay. September 1930.

The Chimney starts from the terrace above the
western gully. The last pitch of 50 feet is the crux. Good
sport can be had in winter.

LEFT EDGE 150 feet SEVERE

J. R. Marshall and I. D. Haig. 9th June 1956.

Go to the left end of the terrace where the north-east edge of the buttress springs up steeply. Climb the slab and groove above to cracked blocks which are turned to the right. 90 feet. Easier climbing to the top.

EAST WALL. There are five steep routes on this wall, which is divided from Blaeberry Rib by the narrow eastern gully. Walk up this grassy gully to reach the routes.

SASSENACH GROOVE 200 feet SEVERE

D. H. Haworth and I. ap E. Hughes. July 1947.

Start in the gully 50 feet up from the Left Edge Route at a prominent groove. Follow the groove, which is sustained.

EAST FACE 150 feet SEVERE

D. H. Haworth and I. McPhail. May 1947.

Half-way up the gully is a prominent cave in the wall of Blaeberry Rib. The cave is the landmark for this and the following three routes.

Start opposite the cave, below the obvious slab of Bollard Slab (see below), make a short right traverse and climb up 15 feet to a grass ledge and spike. Traverse right and downwards into the recessed area to the right of Bollard Slab. Climb a short wall to the left of a shallow chimney with chockstone, and continue by an obvious chimney to the top.

BOLLARD SLAB 135 feet SEVERE
W. Smith and W. Rowney. 8th June 1952.

Start as in previous route, but climb straight up a crack to a grass ledge and block at 25 feet. From the block, follow a line of holds up the attractive slab above to a point near the right edge (where a belay can be taken) and then climb the upper part of the slab slightly leftwards on small holds. Then climb the wall above or a groove to its left.

From the block, an easier line is to traverse right into a groove between two overhangs. Climb the groove and take to the slab when convenient.

NAMELESS WALL 110 feet SEVERE
W. Smith and W. Rowney. 8th June 1952.

Start at a cairn 40 feet left of Bollard Slab at the left edge of a steep wall. Climb for 15 feet, traverse right and follow the thin crack above.

NAMELESS GROOVE 110 feet VERY DIFFICULT
J. R. Marshall and A. H. Hendry. Summer 1953.

Climb the groove immediately left of Nameless Wall.

BLAEBERRY RIB 175 feet VERY DIFFICULT
J. R. Lees, J. G. Parish and R. J. Littlejohn. 24th August 1950.

Immediately east of Lagangarbh Buttress are two very slender ribs, closely parallel. Blaeberry Rib is the westmost rib and contains three pitches, of which two are very difficult.

(The eastmost rib has been climbed but was not worth the effort. It yielded only one severe pitch of 100 feet, followed by a grassy scramble.)

STAIRCASE BUTTRESS

To the east of the two parallel ribs (which lie to the left of Lagangarbh Buttress), but rather higher than them, is the distinctive stepped up formation of Staircase Buttress. Diagram p. 4. The rock is sound and the climbing varied. It is possible to link routes and to make many variations of line and difficulty. Accordingly, the routes described below are, in a sense, arbitrary although worthwhile. Perhaps the best landmark for the start is the cave a little above the lowest rocks near the left flank. Again to the left is a narrow and shallow gully. Routes are described from right to left.

REHABILITATION ROUTE   300 feet
VERY DIFFICULT
J. G. Parish and J. R. Lees. 28th February 1952.

Start at the lowest left-hand rocks, go up a wide crack and move right on to slabs to a large platform. Now go up the wall facing the gully on the west side to a ledge and climb a 10-foot crack and slabs to reach a distinctive grassy platform. The platform is partly separated from the wall beyond by a miniature gap, from which to the right falls a chimney and to the left the final part of the East Chimney Variation described below. Make a right upward traverse on the wall beyond the gap and move round the edge to the open corner and line of weakness above. Climb this line, or, better, the steeper rocks to the left, and reach the foot of a large and prominent diamond-shaped slab at a very easy angle. Walk up the slab to the base of the short, steep wall which skirts the top section of the buttress. This can be breached in a number of places which are obvious, and scrambling follows to the top.

c

ORIGINAL ROUTE   300 feet   VERY DIFFICULT

D. H. Haworth. 20th April 1947.

Look for the cave which is mentioned in the general description of the buttress as being on the left flank. Climb on heather to the cave and make an exit from it on the right wall. Make two left traverses into a gully. Follow the left branch of a chimney, then leave it by the left wall and climb to a grassy terrace overlooking the gully on the left of the buttress. Climb to the top of the buttress.

EAST CHIMNEY VARIATION   VERY DIFFICULT

J. R. Lees and J. G. Parish. 24th February 1952.

This is a variation start to either Rehabilitation Route or Original Route. It cuts across the latter and joins the former at the distinctive grassy platform already described.

Start on an arête left of and below the cave, which is mentioned in the general description of the buttress as being on the left flank. Climb a small chimney to a detached boulder and traverse into the gully on the left (the second of the two left traverses mentioned in Original Route). Now climb the 70-foot East Chimney immediately above. The first 20 feet are often greasy and a little strenuous. This leads to the grassy platform. Now continue by Rehabilitation Route.

WINTER—L. S. Lovat and C. E. Wood. 20th February 1955.

The line taken followed the arête of the East Chimney Variation and then a right traverse on to the Rehabilitation Route. It was severe in places. Time taken 1½ hours.

PEDESTAL ARÊTE   250 feet   SEVERE

J. R. Marshall and L. S. Lovat. 23rd May 1955.

Pedestal Arête is immediately left of and a little higher than the arête of the East Chimney Variation, and is separated from the latter by a gully which narrows to a chimney. The arête joins the final rocks of Staircase Buttress.

Climb numerous blocks and pinnacles to reach a gap beyond a high gendarme. Cross the gap and make a delicate left traverse to the left edge of the vertical crux section. Climb the edge for about ten feet, traverse diagonally rightwards across the face and continue up to a broad grass ledge. Make a pull-up on the short right wall and go to the triangular stance at the left edge of the final wall of Staircase Buttress. Finish round to the left up the very exposed short chimney.

From Staircase Buttress two faces, one above the other, can be seen to the east across the dividing grass slopes. The lower and longer face contains the routes.

HAWKER'S CRACK   100 feet   SEVERE

P. Walsh and C. Vigano. July 1954.

This is an obvious crack near the bottom left end of the face, which is climbed in two pitches of 40 and 60 feet with an awkward move at 25 feet.

PEDLAR'S GROOVE   135 feet   SEVERE

P. Walsh and C. Vigano. July 1954.

Start lower than and left of Hawker's Crack. Climb 10 feet, traverse left and continue steeply for 45 feet to a belay. Step down and right and climb a groove (immediately left of Hawker's Crack) for 80 feet, below the corner of the face.

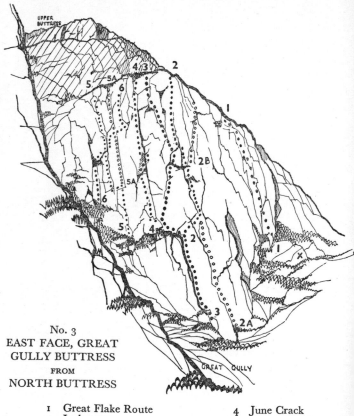

No. 3
EAST FACE, GREAT GULLY BUTTRESS
FROM
NORTH BUTTRESS

1	Great Flake Route	4	June Crack
2	Ledgeway	5	August Crack
2A	Direct Start to Ledgeway	5A	July Crack
2B	Direct Finish to Ledgeway	6	Trident Crack
3	Direct Route and Direct Finish	X	Great Flake

Access to the Great Gully Group is made by the slopes left of the Great Gully, contouring into the gully below Cuneiform Buttress; or better, by the rocks well right of Great Gully, contouring into the gully below Great Gully Buttress.

GREAT GULLY BUTTRESS

This buttress stands on the right of the Great Gully on roughly the same level as Cuneiform Buttress and the West Face of North Buttress. Great Gully is flanked by its east face, which provides by far the best climbing on the buttress and some of the best rock on the mountain.

There are three indifferent routes on the north face.

SUNSET RIB   100 feet   VERY DIFFICULT

I. Dingwall and J. Cunningham. June 1947.

Near the right end of the narrow north face is a thin grey rib to the right of a smooth groove. Climb the rib for 30 feet and continue by easier rocks to the top.

SUNSET GROOVE   130 feet   VERY DIFFICULT

J. Cunningham and I. Dingwall. June 1947.

Ten feet left of Sunset Rib is a groove leading to an obvious short slab below another groove. Follow that line and continue to the top.

GREAT FLAKE ROUTE   150 feet   VERY DIFFICULT

J. Cunningham and I. Dingwall. June 1947.

The Great Flake stands out clearly a few feet to the right of the corner dividing the north and east faces. Begin at a cairn below it and climb the 15 foot arête immediately above the cairn. Climb a pillar bordered by cracks and carry on by grooves to the top.

There are six interesting and sustained routes on the east face (diagram p. 14), of which Ledgeway, Direct Route and June Crack share the same first pitch. About mid-way along the foot of the face, a 40-foot rib abuts against it. The rib is topped by a wide grass ledge. For these three routes, start at the groove to the immediate right of the rib.

LEDGEWAY   200 feet   SEVERE

W. Smith and R. Hope. 7th September 1952.

Climb the groove described, to the grass ledge. Traverse right and up to a shallow, white-scarred fault and follow the fault to a bulge. Pass to the left of the bulge and go up leftwards to another wide grass ledge at 75 feet with a large pointed flake belay. Climb the flake and then the crack and open groove above it for 35 feet to easy ground.

Direct Start   SEVERE

J. R. Marshall. 17th June 1956.

Start a few feet right of and lower than the original start. The fault followed joins the second pitch at the white-scarred section and therefore necessitates a very long run-out unless a small belay be taken on the wall.

Final Variation   80 feet   SEVERE

L. S. Lovat and C. G. M. Slesser. 30th June 1957

In finishing the second pitch a fairly long left traverse is made to the large pointed flake belay. Instead of traversing, climb the obvious crack which springs up from the right-hand end of the grassy ledge. Diagram p. 14.

DIRECT ROUTE 200 feet SEVERE

S. Smith and I. Dingwall. October 1946.

First pitch as for Ledgeway. From the left end of the grass ledge climb up and slightly left for about 15 feet, then make for a rightward sloping shelf. Step up on to the shelf and continue up the fracture above for 60 feet to the stance and pointed flake belay described in Ledgeway. The original final pitch approximates to the final pitch of Ledgeway. To provide a separate finish the following pitch should be climbed:

Direct Finish 85 feet. SEVERE

L. S. Lovat. June 1955.

Climb a short steep wall to the left of the pointed flake and enter a long line of weakness which trends slightly leftwards to the top of the buttress. Diagram p. 14.

JUNE CRACK 200 feet VERY SEVERE

W. Smith and J. Cunningham. 12th June 1948.

First pitch as for Ledgeway. From the left end of the grass ledge climb up and slightly left for about 15 feet to reach a very prominent crack. Climb the crack, embarking on the left wall eventually and in 45 feet gain a small rock shelf and belay. Above this the crack overhangs; enter it, climb the nose to the right for a few feet. The subsequent move left into the crack is the crux of the route. Continue up the crack, distinctly delicate in places, and reach a belay at 80 feet. Finish in a further 20 feet of easier climbing. Diagram p. 14.

JULY CRACK   160 feet   VERY SEVERE

R. Smith and A. Frazer. June 1958.

Near the left end of the east face, a right-angled grassy groove can be seen above a 40-foot slab, split by three thin fissures which mark the start of Trident Crack. July Crack and August Crack share the same first pitch 35 feet down to the right, at a grass ledge with cairn.

Climb up for 40 feet to a stance and belay below a thin crack. Climb the crack. Diagram p. 14.

AUGUST CRACK   165 feet   VERY SEVERE

W. Smith and J. Cunningham. 3rd August 1955.

Following the first pitch common to July Crack, make a leftward descending traverse for 15 feet to a thin crack, which climb to a stance and belay. Directly above is a steep fault running slightly leftwards. Climb the fault, negotiating some loose blocks, for 60 feet to finish. Diagram p. 14.

TRIDENT CRACK   150 feet   SEVERE

W. Smith and J. Cunningham. 3rd August 1955.

The description of the start of this route has been made under July Crack.

Climb the thin fissure and go up the slab to a large grass ledge at 40 feet. Continue by a wide crack to the right of the right-angled grassy groove above, and in 20 feet reach a stance and belay, common to August Crack. This route now cuts rightwards across the line of August Crack and the last pitch has a 90-foot run-out. Step down a little, traverse right for 20 feet, move up a steep fault with some loose flakes, and finish by slabs. Diagram p. 14.

GREAT GULLY UPPER BUTTRESS

This buttress is seen well above Great Gully Buttress. Diagram p. 14. It presents to Great Gully a short, steep face which is in fact the east face of Broad Buttress above the exit of Narrow Gully. There are four routes.

BENT CRACK RIB   135 feet   VERY DIFFICULT

C. E. Wood and C. Ford. 15th May 1954.

At the north-east corner of the face there is a very prominent crack with a rightward twist near the top. This route follows the rib to the immediate right of the crack.

BENT CRACK   130 feet   VERY DIFFICULT

C. E. Wood and C. Ford. 15th May 1954.

Climb the crack described in the previous route.

FAÇADE   140 feet   VERY DIFFICULT

L. S. Lovat. 30th June 1957.

Some distance along the east face proper, there is an open corner at the base, to the right of May Crack described immediately below. Start up the wall to the immediate right of the corner and take the line of least resistance for about 70 feet to a long horizontal fault below overhangs. Aim right for a breach in the form of a vertical groove. Climb the groove and trend left on the steep wall above to finish in a further 70 feet.

MAY CRACK 140 feet VERY SEVERE

R. Hope and W. Smith. 17th May 1952.

Mid-way along the east face proper and about 60 feet up the face, an obvious right-angled corner will be seen. Twenty feet right of this is a definite crack, which is very thin in the lower part of the face. The route follows the crack in two pitches of 70 feet. Step off a detached block and go up for 40 feet till a long reach has to be made for a satisfactory hold. Use the left wall where necessary in the next 30 feet. Keep in the crack in the second pitch.

GREAT GULLY 1200 feet EASY

Norman Collie. 1894.

A big pitch near the foot of North Buttress and a dirty 80-foot pitch near the foot of Cuneiform Buttress can be avoided. The last 500-foot slope is straightforward.
WINTER—Under thin snow the gully may be found difficult and in icy conditions may become very difficult at the 80-foot pitch. Under heavy snow the gully may become a walk. Diagram p. 4.

CUNEIFORM BUTTRESS

This buttress lies high up in Great Gully against the west wall of North Buttress, from which it is separated by the great chimney of Raven's Gully. There are three routes and one direct finish. A great deal of the rock becomes particularly greasy when wet. Diagram p. 24.

OVERHANGING GROOVE 230 feet SEVERE

D. Stevens and I. Provan. April 1955.

The west face of Cuneiform Buttress terminates to the south where a small buttress abuts against it. Near the small buttress, a corner leads into a groove. This is the line of the route.

Climb the corner to a belay below an overhang at 50 feet. Traverse left and down into a crack, climb the overhanging crux and go up to a small cave with a thread belay at 40 feet. Continue up the groove for 40 feet, avoid the overhang by the right wall and finish in another 100 feet by easy slabs.

THE LONG CHIMNEY   450 feet   SEVERE

D. Stevens and Miss D. M. Lawrie. May 1955.

Start at the lowest rocks near the entrance of Raven's Gully and follow the line of least resistance to reach a broad grassy terrace. So far the route is the same as the original route next described. Now traverse hard right and up into a long shallow chimney, which is an obvious feature of the buttress. Continue up the chimney to reach a break with a slab on the left. Climb a little chimney, make a step right and continue up the wall to the top of the buttress. Diagram p. 24.

WINTER—R. Smith and D. Leaver. 15th December 1957.

The Ordinary Route was followed to above the short, steep pitch beyond the broad, grassy terrace. A right traverse was then made into the Long Chimney which was followed to the top. The route was occasionally severe and took 4-5 hours.

ORDINARY ROUTE   450 feet   VERY DIFFICULT

J. H. B. Bell and A. Harrison. June 1930.

Start at the lowest rocks near the entrance of Raven's Gully and follow the line of least resistance to reach a broad grassy terrace. From the right end of the terrace climb a short, steep pitch and follow again the line of least resistance by grassy grooves to another broad ledge under the vertical upper third of the buttress. Traverse to the right round an exposed corner on to the west face. Climb an obvious shelf, above which the route turns into the centre of the cliff. This last section from the broad ledge gives a splendid finish of only difficult standard. Diagram p. 24.

WINTER—J. R. Marshall, D. N. Mill and G. J. Ritchie. 15th December 1957.

The Ordinary Route was followed throughout and was severe at the summer crux and at the west shelf near the top. Time taken 4-5 hours.

THE CENTRAL CHIMNEY   110 feet   SEVERE

E. A. M. Wedderburn and J. H. B. Bell. September 1934.

This is a direct finish to the Ordinary Route. From the broad ledge under the vertical upper third of the buttress, traverse left to the foot of a very prominent chimney. Climb vegetation for 50 feet to reach a cave with belay. Proceed on steep rock and reach the top of the buttress in a further 60 feet. This last pitch is sustained and finely situated, although on dubious rock.

RAVEN'S GULLY   450 feet   VERY SEVERE

J. B. Nimlin, B. Braithwaite, N. Millar, J. Macfarlane, and A. N. Other. June 1937.

From the Glencoe road, Raven's Gully is seen as a dark, vertical slit dividing the Cuneiform Buttress from North Buttress. Diagram p. 24. It is a climb of character and variety and has eleven pitches from 15 to 60 feet in height, of which only one is easy. Dry weather is desirable as the whole route becomes readily greasy.

Pitch 4 is the crux. It forms a double tier with pitch 3, of total height 30 feet. The crux begins at the midway cave (good belay) and presents an awkward 15-foot pitch. Climb on the left wall until it is possible to use a high right hand-hold above the slot between the wall and the overhang. Keep well out in pulling over the top. There is a belay well up the easy-angle scree above this pitch. At this point an escape can be made on to Cuneiform Buttress.

Pitch 5 includes a wriggle on to a mid-way chockstone and a deceptive open groove above.

Pitch 6 is 60 feet in length and is climbed on the left wall. The first 30 feet are on small holds and severe.

Above pitch 8 a huge crag arches the gully, which a little way further rears up in splendid caves and over-hangs. At the top of pitch 8 a rib and shelf rise steeply against the wall of North Buttress. Traverse left round the foot of the rib into grooves running parallel with the gully. Climb 150 feet of easier rock to a grass platform at the edge of the gully and above the caves of the Direct Finish. Finish by a narrow and artificial 10-foot chimney or by traversing left across slabs and climbing a 40-foot chimney and fold.

Direct Finish   VERY SEVERE

J. Cunningham, W. Smith and T. Paul. 30th May 1948.

At the top of pitch 8, instead of traversing left continue straight up the gully to the chockstones and caves. Climb first on the right wall, traverse on to the left wall and gain a dark cave. Straddle until rocky shelves allow a left traverse under huge chockstones to a grass ledge, which gives access to the ordinary route at the second last pitch.

This finish is sustained and harder than the crux of

No. 4
WEST
FACE

NORTH BUTTRESS and
CUNEIFORM BUTTRESS

1 Ordinary Route: Cuneiform
  Buttress
2 The Long Chimney
3 Central Chimney   5 Shibboleth
4 Guerdon Grooves   6 Bludger's Route

7 Belial   10 Bloody Crack   13 Doom Arête
8 Pluto   11 Revelation   R.G. Raven's Gully
9 Girdle Traverse 12 Nightmare traverse G.G.B. Great Gully Buttress
      + +   Direct Finish, Bludger's Route

the ordinary route. The straddling becomes increasingly strenuous.

WINTER—H. McInnes and C. Bonington. 14th February 1953.

This ascent, of the ordinary route, took 6½ hours and was very severe. Pitch 4 took 1½ hours. Two pitons were used on it and crampons were worn. Socks were then used until the final slopes when crampons were again worn. The chockstone in Pitch 5 was lassoed, saving much time in the icy conditions. Two pitons were used on Pitch 6 and a further two pitons were used as belays in other places.

Conditions are seldom favourable for a winter ascent and at least two previous attempts were thwarted by the time consumed in dealing with exceptional difficulties of ice and verglas. It seems likely that ideal conditions for a magnificent climb would involve a complete transformation by a heavy plaster of snow and ice, when pitches such as the summer crux would be banked up. In any conditions an easy climb can scarcely be envisaged and the final 190 feet might be very formidable.

WEST FACE OF NORTH BUTTRESS

The remaining feature of the Great Gully Group is the West Face of North Buttress. This face has an evil tilt and takes a long time to dry. In fine conditions, it affords really interesting and exposed climbing, much of which is also very severe. Apart from an area parallel to and above Raven's Gully (the line of Guerdon Grooves), the face is actually divided into two tiers. It is proposed first to describe, from right to left as usual, the routes which begin on the lower tier, that is, from Great Gully, and then similarly to describe the routes which begin on the upper tier. Diagram p. 24.

GUERDON GROOVES   540 feet   VERY SEVERE

J. Cunningham and W. Smith. 13th June 1948.

A run-out of 150 feet is involved in this route. Start at a cairn 20 feet below Raven's Gully. Climb a series of grooves trending rightwards to reach some large flakes at 90 feet. Traverse 10 feet horizontally right round an awkward square-cut corner and take a belay. (If a belay is not taken here the leader is out of view and the run-out exceeds 150 feet.) Climb a groove immediately above moving slightly left and as soon as possible traverse right into a groove overlooking the gully. Climb this groove. The route is not easy to find. The groove ends at a projecting nose and a crack on the left should then be climbed leading to a slab and so to a small grass ledge with a belay and a cairn. Traverse right across a grassy corner into a fault with an overhanging top. Climb the fault until an easy traverse can be made to a belay near Raven's Gully. Easy rocks follow for 200 feet to a large terrace level with the top of Raven's Gully. Diagram p. 24.

SHIBBOLETH   550 feet   VERY SEVERE

R. Smith and A. Frazer. June 1958.

This is the most direct line up the whole cliff. Climb the first pitch of Guerdon Grooves to the large flakes at 90 feet. Climb 20 feet by a crack on the left, traverse left 10 feet and go up right to reach a very prominent groove. Go up the groove, using a piton at 50 feet, and make a piton belay. Continue up the groove, step right at the top and go up and left to the belay below the flake crack on Revelation at 70 feet. Now, go up and right for 50 feet to a jug-handle, traverse hard left for 10 feet and climb to a stance below the left end of an overhang. Climb the overhanging corner above and cross Girdle Traverse to a belay at 100 feet. Climb up and then left to gain a shallow, overhanging corner, which follow to a ledge on the right and piton belay at 70 feet. The final pitch is 120 feet. Climb the wall above and trend rightwards by grooves to a platform. Finish by an overhanging corner. Diagram p. 24.

BLUDGER'S ROUTE   160 feet   VERY SEVERE

P. Walsh, H. McInnes and T. Laurie. 21st September 1952.

The line of the first part of this route can be seen from any point near the foot of Guerdon Grooves, i.e. about 20 feet or so down from Raven's Gully. It goes straight up a steep fracture to a small rock ledge below an overhanging section and avoids the latter by a left traverse, as described below.

Start at a corner almost directly below the fracture and about 35 feet left of and below Raven's Gully. Climb to a belay below the vertical section of the fracture. The next pitch to the rock ledge and flake belay is strenuous, sustained and occasionally overhanging. Climb by a detached flake to the right of the groove, then step left into the groove. Go up the groove to the rock ledge. Holds are mainly good and two pitons are in position. From the rock ledge traverse left along a ledge to the corner. Go round the corner, continue the traverse delicately for a few feet and descend a steep wall to the base of a large recess. Now climb a 20-foot chimney on the left to reach the terrace of the upper tier. Diagram p. 24.

D

Direct Finish   100 feet   VERY SEVERE

J. R. Marshall, J. Griffin, G. Adams and R. Marshall.
    July 1957.

This finish has the merit of connecting Bludger's
Route (above) to the start of Revelation. (See p. 29.)

Move left along the rock ledge to the corner, as described above. Instead of going round the corner and
traversing, climb the corner for 5 feet, traverse left into
a vertical crack and follow this to a ledge and corner;
move round the edge on to the wall and climb on excellent slabby rock, finishing by a left move on to the belay
of Revelation.

This combination of Bludger's Route and Revelation
makes a sustained line up the whole cliff. Diagram p. 24.

BELIAL   160 feet   VERY DIFFICULT

J. H. B. Bell and J. R. Wood. September 1940.

Start 60 feet below the foot of Raven's Gully. Climb
50 feet trending leftwards to a grass stance. From this
point take as direct a line as possible and eventually
enter the rightmost of two parallel 20-foot chimneys.
The leftmost chimney is easier but more loose. There is
a cairn above the rightmost chimney, marking the end
of the route, which is below the start of the upper tier
routes. Diagram p. 24.

PLUTO   160 feet   SEVERE

E. R. Zenthon and B. V. Fox. May 1940.

Start at a cairn 150 feet below the foot of Raven's
Gully and level with a large detached block in Great
Gully. The route follows a line of weakness to the right
of a large tower set against the face. Climb 5 feet to a
slab, traverse left under a bulge and make for a grass

platform at 30 feet. Now climb a narrow, 10-foot
chimney, formed by a big detached flake, to another
grass platform and belay. The crux above goes 40 feet
by a corner and crack to a triangular ledge. It is often
greasy and can be avoided by a severe deviation on the
right, finishing at the same point. From the ledge either
climb straight up a short overhang and steep rocks to
finish or traverse left and climb a shallow groove for
80 feet. The upper tier is above. Diagram p. 24.

REVELATION 290 feet VERY SEVERE

P. Walsh and C. Vigano. June 1956.

Just above and to the right of Belial's finish there is
a block belay and an easy rightward sloping ledge.
Follow the ledge round the corner and go up and right
for a few feet. Move left and up a steep groove till a
ledge is reached at 100 feet. Belay. Swing down from
belay into a steep groove which follow for 20 feet. Make
a very severe traverse right to a flake crack. Use undercut holds on the flake, swing into the crack and climb up
to a poor stance and small chockstone belay below an
overhang (80 feet). Avoid on the left and go up 40 feet
to block belay. The fourth pitch of 70 feet follows the
crest of a large flake to the right and so by easy climbing
to a deep corner with a belay at the back. Diagram p. 24.

DOOM ARÊTE 230 feet VERY SEVERE

P. Walsh and C. Vigano. June 1956.

Climb Pitch 1 of Revelation. Go back along the ledge
from the belay for a few feet and climb a steep wall
aiming left for the edge and so up to a shallow corner.
Start up the corner, then step left (crux) and continue
to a ledge and above to a small grass ledge. Piton belay

10 feet above. Run-out 80 feet and very exposed. Pitch 3 (60 feet) goes up to the piton and by a right traverse round a very exposed corner to a crack, which is climbed to a ledge and then a corner and so to the finish. Diagram p. 24.

NIGHTMARE TRAVERSE 260 feet VERY SEVERE

P. Walsh and M. Noon. July 1956.

Pitch 1, 120 feet, starts 15 feet below Revelation. Traverse across an arête and to the left of a small overhang; make an awkward move to the right round a corner and so across to a flake and a piton belay. Pitch 2 is also 120 feet. Climb up the rib above till a hard traverse can be made to the right on to small ledges. Climb a crack for 10 feet and then climb 20 feet to the top of a steep wall and small spike. Insert a piton and descend an overhang with aid of rope to a flake belay. Climb a crack above for 20 feet to a small ledge and belay. Now the climb joins the finish of Guerdon Grooves. Diagram p. 24.

BLOODY CRACK 130 feet VERY SEVERE

P. Walsh and S. Crawford. June 1956.

Start about 25 feet left of Revelation at the foot of a 130-foot crack. Climb the crack for 60 feet to a grass ledge (flake belay 6 feet left). Very strenuous. Go back into the crack and climb it to the top. Diagram p. 24.

GIRDLE TRAVERSE 460 feet VERY SEVERE

P. Walsh and C. Vigano. June 1956.

Left of Bloody Crack there is another crack. The Girdle Traverse starts up the wall left of the latter crack until a step is made across the crack on to a ledge which is followed to a flake belay at 60 feet. Continue right along the ledge to a corner with a small triangular grass ledge a few feet higher. Ten feet above that take a piton belay at 40 feet. The third pitch is also 40 feet. Above the piton traverse right round a very exposed corner and continue past a crack to below a small ledge. Go up to the ledge and along to huge flake belays. Pitch 5 (70 feet) goes gradually up and right, using a piton runner, to gain a sloping ledge and a block. Belay by a piton in the crack above the block. Another 70-foot pitch follows. Traverse right to a grassy corner and then up 30 feet to a belay below a large cave. Now descend a few feet and follow a line of weakness beside Raven's Gully for 100 feet to a belay in a corner well up Guerdon Grooves. The final pitch of 70 feet goes right and up to the top of North Buttress. Diagram p. 24.

THE NORTH-EAST FACE

The North-East Face comprises four Buttresses and three gullies. These, from right to left as viewed from the Glencoe Road, are North Buttress, Crowberry Gully, Crowberry Ridge, Easy Gully, Curved Ridge, D Gully and D Gully Buttress. (The north face of Central Buttress is, for convenience, described under the heading "The South-East Face".) Diagram p. 4.

NORTH BUTTRESS

This 1000-foot buttress falls north-north-east from the summit. It is the huge rounded mass to the east of Great Gully. The lower 300 feet lie at a fairly high angle but beyond that the angle eases greatly. From a point below and left of Pluto on the West Face to a point right of Gallows Route on the East Face, the buttress can be

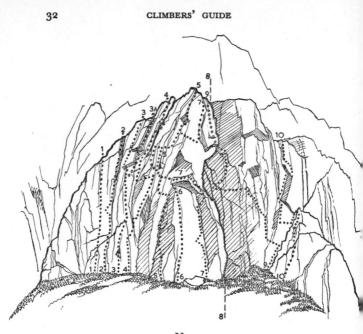

No. 5

EAST FACE, NORTH BUTTRESS FROM BELOW BOTTLENECK CHIMNEY

1   Brevity Crack
2   Shackle Route
3   Shattered Crack
3A Variation Shattered Crack
4   Crow's Nest Crack
5   Mainbrace Crack
6   Bogtrotter
7   White Wall Crack
8   Bottleneck Chimney
9   Pendulum
10 Gallows Route

climbed almost anywhere by moderate lines of great variety. The original route is described below.

WEST ROUTE   1000 feet   MODERATE

W. Brown, — Rose, and W. Tough. July 1895.

Start at the centre of the buttress and climb to the foot of the steep section. Traverse right to near the edge of Great Gully and take the easiest line above. A prominent leftward sloping chimney is a feature. Diagram p. 4.

NORTH BUTTRESS IN WINTER

Under heavy snow or in icy conditions, North Buttress can be at least very difficult. Good sport can be had in many of the chimneys and cracks which may be filled with ice or covered with verglas. A great variety of conditions may be encountered and much time spent. Keeping to the open walls, particularly on the west face, will usually save time.

EAST FACE OF NORTH BUTTRESS

This very attractive face varies between 300 and 350 feet in height and overlooks Crowberry Gully. Diagrams pp. 32 and 34. It is skirted at the base by a wide terrace (The Terrace); it is crossed about the middle by a shallow grass gully (Green Gully), which declines to the right and ends as such in the region of the exit of Bottleneck Chimney; and it is encircled near the top by a broad ledge (High Ledge), which connects Crowberry Gully and Great Gully. The routes which begin at The Terrace will be described first, from right to left. The section from Gallows Route to and including Shattered Crack is the steepest and most sustained part of the Face and is in clearer relief in the diagram on p. 32.

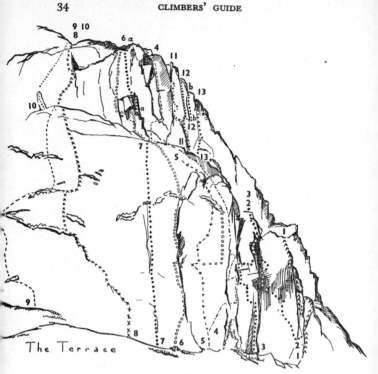

No. 6

EAST FACE, NORTH BUTTRESS FROM THE TERRACE

1	Gallows Route	7	Brevity Crack
2	Pendulum	8	Slanting Groove
3	Mainbrace Crack	9	N.E. Zigzag
4	Crow's Nest Crack	10	Judas Rib
5	Shattered Crack	11	Hangman's Crack
5	0000: Variation	12	Guillotine
6	Shackle Route	12B	Gibbet
6A	Alternate Finish	13	Garrotte

GALLOWS ROUTE   130 feet   VERY SEVERE

J. Cunningham and I. Dingwall. June 1947.

The Terrace is terminated on the right by a broad nose projecting from the Face. Immediately right of the corner thus formed is a shallow chimney, which is the first pitch.

Climb the chimney 40 feet to a belay. Descend 10 feet and traverse left 10 feet to reach a very steep scoop. The traverse is very awkward. Climb the scoop, surmounting the overhang on the left, then another scoop, turning another overhang on the right by a shelf. A third steep scoop is climbed until a left traverse can be made to better holds and so to a stance and belay. This whole section is sustained and strenuous. Easy scrambling above leads to Green Gully. Diagrams pp. 32 and 34.

PENDULUM   130 feet   VERY SEVERE

P. Walsh and J. Cunningham. August 1955.

Use the same start as Gallows Route and at a point about 15 feet below the traverse of that Route traverse left 8 feet to a crack. A piton was used on the next section. Climb the crack and then the right side of a small mossy slab on to a sloping ledge, from which traverse left to a stance and belay. This first pitch, of 65 feet, is both very strenuous and delicate. Now lasso a large flake above to the right, swing over, climb the rope and mantelshelf on to the top of the flake. Quit the flake early because it is loose. Go up a few feet, traverse across the very obvious chimney to the left (Bottleneck Chimney, described below) and finish by climbing a fault on the left wall leading to Green Gully. Diagrams pp. 32 and 34.

BOTTLENECK CHIMNEY   130 feet   SEVERE
R. G. Donaldson and G. R. B. McCarter. Summer 1941.

This dark recess, shaped like a bottle, is about twenty feet left of the broad nose of Gallows Route and of the right extremity of The Terrace. It is an obvious landmark, even from the Glencoe Road.

The recess contains a crack, varying in width, which affords a rather strenuous climb for 70 feet to the overhang of the "bottleneck". Traverse right by high hand-holds, exit through the neck and climb easy rocks to Green Gully. Diagram p. 32.

HANGMAN'S CRACK   100 feet   VERY SEVERE
R. G. Donaldson and G. R. B. McCarter. Summer 1941.

As this route was first climbed as the natural continuation of the Bottleneck Chimney line above Green Gully, it will be described here for convenience, together with, from left to right, three short routes to its immediate right.

Hangman's Crack is a clean-cut, steep and very prominent dièdre, about 50 feet above and slightly right of the finish of Bottleneck Chimney. Climb 30 feet of moderate rock to reach a sloping ledge and belay at the base of the crack. Go up a few feet slightly right and make an awkward mantelshelf move, which is the crux. Traverse left into the crack and follow it until a severe traverse and long stretch is made on to the right wall. Steep climbing remains to the top. Diagram p. 34.

GARROTTE   100 feet   VERY SEVERE
J. Cunningham and M. Noon. 4th August 1955.

Ten feet right of Hangman's Crack is an obvious thin crack. Climb this crack for 70 feet to a grass stance without belay. A piton was inserted as a runner at 40 feet where there is a nook, as the crux section is above the piton. The final 30 feet above the grass stance involves an overhang but is not so strenuous and leads to easy ledges. Diagram p. 34.

GIBBET   95 feet   VERY SEVERE

E. Taylor and W. Smith. 9th September 1956.

Climb Garrotte to the first bulge and traverse delicately right into a clean-cut groove. Climb the groove, using a piton at 10 feet, to the top. Diagram p. 34.

GUILLOTINE   95 feet   VERY SEVERE

W. Smith and T. Paul. 4th August 1955.

Start at a cairn 30 feet right of Garrotte. Climb an overhanging wall with a thin crack (piton in place) and make an awkward move on to a small shelf at 25 feet. Bear left on the groove above to finish. Diagram p. 34.

WHITE WALL CRACK   165 feet   VERY SEVERE

W. Smith and G. McIntosh. August 1955.

The left bounding wall of Bottleneck Chimney is distinctively white-scarred. Climb a thin crack near the right edge of the wall and insert two pitons at 30 feet to reach a pull-up on to a sloping ledge with a large flake. Make a long step right to a rib, which is climbed to a ledge at 75 feet. A belay can be arranged. Traverse left round a corner and continue the traverse for 20 feet to reach an open groove. Follow the groove, which leads to a left traverse for 6 feet to a belay. (The groove and belay are on Mainbrace Crack, described below.) About 40 feet of rope has been run out on this second pitch, a great deal of which consists of traversing. Climb a wide crack above for about 15 feet and traverse right to a small ledge below an arête—the section to the ledge is

also part of Mainbrace Crack. Now make an awkward
step down, traverse right for 15 feet to a rib and climb
up to Green Gully. 90 feet. Diagram p. 32.

BOGTROTTER   75 feet (to join Bottleneck Chimney)
E. Taylor and W. Smith. June 1957.   UNCLASSIFIED

This route follows the line of the cracked arête forming
a corner between White Wall Crack and Mainbrace
Crack, about 6 feet left of the former. Eleven pitons
were used in reaching the ledge about 75 feet up, below
the overhang. A rightward traverse was then made into
the neck of Bottleneck Chimney. (An avoiding move to
the left had to be made to reach a poor stance and a high
flake belay before making the rightward traverse.)

This initial pitch is climbed almost solely by artificial
technique. Any free climbing is about severe. The rock
is shattered. Diagram p. 32.

MAINBRACE CRACK   165 feet   VERY SEVERE
P. Walsh and W. Smith. August 1955.

Round the corner some yards left of Bottleneck
Chimney and White Wall Crack, and on the true east
face, is a small overhung recess and an obvious shattered
fault. Start a few feet to the right of this fault at a groove
and climb it, surmounting an overhang at 10 feet and
gaining a crack. Go up the crack 30 feet then quit the
groove to traverse up and left for about 12 feet to an
open groove. Follow the groove, which leads to a left
traverse for 6 feet to a belay at 80 feet. (This belay is
just above the long upward step on Crow's Nest Crack,
described below.) Climb a wide crack above for about
15 feet and traverse right to a small ledge below an
arête. Finish up the arête to reach Green Gully. Diagrams pp. 32 and 34.

CROW'S NEST CRACK   285 feet   VERY SEVERE

J. Cunningham and P. McGonigle. June 1946.

The general line of this route is by a long, narrow crack, which springs from a small overhung recess 12 yards left of Bottleneck Chimney and round the corner from it on the east face. It should not be confused with Shackle Route which follows the very prominent wide crack about four yards to the left. In addition, although this route begins very near Shattered Crack it soon trends rightwards away from the line of that route, maintaining a course between the latter and Mainbrace Crack to the immediate right.

Start 3 yards left of the overhung recess (where Mainbrace Crack starts) at a V-shaped cavity and go up for 10 feet. Continue slightly right for 25 feet, make an awkward step at a corner and traverse right into the narrow crack. Twenty feet up make a delicate move on to a slab on the left. The next 15-foot section is the crux. Then regain the crack where it is divided by an overhanging nose. Follow the left-hand crack to Green Gully.

Above Green Gully the route continues for about 120 feet to High Ledge. At the lower right end of Green Gully there is a tall pinnacle-flake with a jammed block between it and the left wall. From the black groove to the right of the pinnacle-flake, climb up rightwards to an obvious crack springing up for 100 feet to High Ledge. Climb the crack. Diagrams pp. 32 and 34.

SHATTERED CRACK   165 feet   VERY SEVERE

J. Cunningham and P. McGonigle. June 1946.

The line of the route is by a long thin crack, 15 yards left of Bottleneck Chimney, a few feet left of Crow's

Nest Crack and three yards right of the very prominent wide crack of Shackle Route.

Start immediately left of the V-shaped cavity of Crow's Nest Crack and go straight up the steep wall above on good holds, passing a large, loose flake. Find a small belay somewhere below the block overhangs well above, or traverse left below these into the sentry-box of Shackle Route and belay there. The crack splits the block overhang and the crux involves a few feet of careful climbing on small holds. Steep, pleasant climbing remains to Green Gully. Diagrams pp. 32 and 34.

Left Crack Variation   VERY SEVERE

W. Smith. 1952.

When the block overhangs are reached, it will be seen that there is another thin crack splitting them to the left of Shattered Crack. Climb it.

SHACKLE ROUTE   165 feet   VERY DIFFICULT

S. H. Cross and Miss A. M. Nelson. June 1936.

The wide crack of Shackle Route is a landmark for the whole section of the Face left of Bottleneck Chimney and it provides a pleasant, classic climb. It is far more obvious than Shattered Crack, which is about 3 yards to the right.

Climb the crack until it is necessary at 60 feet to embark on the left wall for a few feet to reach a "sentry-box" and belay. The move on the left wall is the crux. Continue up the crack and then easy rocks to Green Gully.

Directly above is a tall pinnacle-flake with a jammed block between it and the left wall. Either climb the black groove to the right of the pinnacle, followed by a leftward slanting groove, a steep wall and easier rock to

High Ledge; or climb up to and over the jammed block
to join the leftward slanting groove and so on; or climb
to below the jammed block and traverse out left below
a bulge to gain easier rock leading to High Ledge. The
latter alternative avoids the best sport. Diagrams pp.
32 and 34.

BREVITY CRACK   165 feet   VERY SEVERE

P. Walsh and C. Vigano. Summer 1954.

About 10 feet left of Shackle Route and about 15 feet
up the wall, a thin crack will be seen with a small spike
below it. Climb easily up to the crack and much less
easily up the crack. The mantelshelf on to a sloping
ledge a few feet up the crack is awkward and is the crux.
Higher up, a piton belay will be found about level with
the "sentry-box" of Shackle Route. Steep but easier
climbing follows to Green Gully. Diagrams pp. 32
and 34.

SLANTING GROOVE   340 feet   VERY DIFFICULT

H. W. Grant and P. L. McGeoch. June 1940.

About 10 feet left of Shackle Route and below the
crack of Brevity Crack, a groove slanting leftwards is
easily seen. Follow it to a small ledge then strike up
directly to a large block belay, which is easily turned on
the right. Go straight up to Green Gully. Twenty feet
below the top of Green Gully, climb a crack followed by
black and slabby rock, then trend right by a steep rib
to a ledge below a shattered overhang which is avoided
on the left.

The route described is quite arbitrary. Above the
initial slanting groove, which is the crux, one can climb
anywhere. Diagram p. 34.

NORTH-EAST ZIGZAG   155 feet   DIFFICULT

P. L. McGeoch and H. W. Grant. June 1940.

Rising from the left end of The Terrace, is an obvious
narrow and long rock ledge. Go up left and round a
corner at the end of this ledge to a grass niche and so
by a short, right traverse up to a grass ledge. Trend up
rightwards to the large block of Slanting Groove and then
leftwards to reach Green Gully.

Go to the top of Green Gully, where a narrow and
prominent rib abuts against the face. Climb the rib, go
slightly rightwards and follow any line above to High
Ledge. This latter section above Green Gully was
previously treated as a separate route known as Judas
Rib, but is more truly a continuation of North-East
Zigzag. The standard is difficult. Diagram p. 34.

Variation (section below Green Gully)   155 feet
·   VERY DIFFICULT

J. Mason, G. K. Armstrong and E. Furness. 9th March
1952.

From the grass ledge above the corner, aim for a
prominent detached flake some distance above. Climb
the right edge of the flake and follow any line above it
to Green Gully.

Like Slanting Groove, North-East Zigzag and its
variation are quite arbitrary lines on a section of the
face where the climber can move about as he chooses.
Diagram p. 34.

WINTER—J. R. Marshall, A. H. Hendry and G. J.
Ritchie. Winter 1957.

This ascent went by the line of North-East Zigzag,
joined Slanting Groove upper section and followed

Green Gully leftwards to the series of gullies in the area of East Ribs. It then followed those gullies. Difficulties were mainly found at the start.

EAST RIBS   700 feet   DIFFICULT

Newbigging, Morrison and Burns. April 1905.

At the extreme left of the East Face, the lower and upper tiers are split by wide chimneys. Between the chimneys and Crowberry Gully to the left are the ribs. Start in Crowberry Gully and follow the line of the ribs to High Ledge. Variations are endless.

WINTER—This line is interesting and varied. Difficulties are mainly at the start.

CROWBERRY GULLY   1000 feet   VERY DIFFICULT
(by Right Fork)

F. Greig, H. Raeburn, S. M. Cumming and D. H. Menzies. September 1910.

This magnificent, deep-cut gully divides North Buttress from Crowberry Ridge. Diagrams pp. 4 and 46. As a summer route it is entertaining but not distinguished.

The best route of approach from the west is up the lowest left-hand rocks of North Buttress. From the east the best route is by the waterslide below Curved Ridge. See diagram p. 4.

There are eight principal pitches. The first is a deep cave overhung by an immense boulder. Start well below the cave on the North Buttress wall and climb until a little above the top of the boulder, where a ledge can be traversed left and slightly downwards into the gully-bed.

Four short pitches follow, of which Pitch 5 has interest.

E

Pitch 6 is the well-known Thincrack Chimney. The route goes up the constricting interior and out by a window formed by a jammed stone. Position can be maintained by lung expansion only. The open slabs to the right of the chimney offer normal climbing as an alternative.

The gully forks immediately above. The right fork is the original route, finishing nearer the summit than the left fork, although less interesting, and is described first. Climb straight up from the exit of Thincrack Chimney to join a scree-slope leading to the cave pitch. (The original route at this point was to climb a short pitch in the left fork to a jammed block and traverse right over a saddle into the scree-slope, but this is unnecessary.)

The cave pitch has a high overhanging roof and is climbed near the back by the mossy right wall.

A short easy pitch beyond ends the Gully at a point midway between the Crowberry Tower Gap and the summit. Diagram p. 46.

LEFT FORK   120 feet   SEVERE

B. N. Simmonds and A. C. Marriott. September 1943.

From the exit of Thincrack Chimney, climb one short pitch in the Left Fork. The gully now rises as a vertical chimney roofed by a large capstone. Climb well inside the chimney to reach a constricted stance of jammed stones. Belay (or better, runner, to avoid inconvenience). The next few feet to the cavity below the capstone are severe. There is no proper stance in the cavity, but it is not difficult to attach a runner. Traverse out back and foot for a few feet below the capstone and move round and over it with care, as there is no jughandle above. The situation is excellent. Walk up the narrow cleft beyond to the Crowberry Tower Gap. Diagram p. 46.

CENTRE RIB   140 feet   VERY DIFFICULT

L. S. Lovat. 18th November 1956.

Climb the rib dividing the left and right forks. It is exposed and loose near the top.

WINTER (by Right Fork)—W. M. MacKenzie, J. B. Russell, J. F. Hamilton and J. K. W. Dunn. 9th February 1936.

It is as a natural winter climb that Crowberry Gully is known, not for special difficulty but for beauty, character and length. There are many harder winter gullies in Glencoe and elsewhere, but Crowberry Gully offers, in most winters, all the qualities for a great climb.

Conditions can vary remarkably and in a short time, but the best opportunities are normally in late February and March. There are seldom more than five pitches, some or all of which may be obliterated by a heavy snowfall. Safety and/or time may be affected greatly by the state of the snow between pitches.

The crux is usually the junction of the right and left forks. The summer route is rarely climbable and the best winter route is across the slabs on the right. A coating of snow-ice is required for the traverse, which failing, the scoop between the summer route and the slabs should be tried. The jammed block in the left fork should then provide a belay.

Though the junction is often the criterion of success, the hardest pitch technically may be the cave pitch. It is invariably of pure ice and is sometimes 40 feet.

In certain conditions, one disagreeable feature of the climb may consist of powder-snow avalanches coming off North Buttress. This should be watched for, particularly about the junction and beyond it.

The climb is normally in the severe class but may

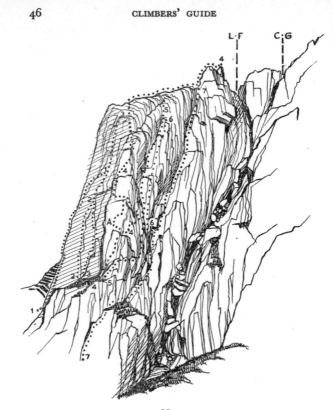

No. 7

CROWBERRY RIDGE, NORTH AND NORTH-EAST FACES

1	Grooved Arête	6	Hyphen Rib
2	Engineer's Crack	7	Shelf Route
3	Fracture Route	A	Abraham's Direct Variation
4	Crowberry Ridge: Direct Route	C.G.	Crowberry Gully
5	Naismith's Route	L.F.	Crowberry Gully Left Fork

vary up or down. Six to ten hours are normally taken. The gully has been climbed in hard conditions in 2½ hours, which is very fast. Parties vary as much as conditions.

WINTER BY LEFT FORK—C. M. G. Smith, R. J. Taunton and I. C. Robertson. 18th March 1949.

Very little is known about this ascent. From the nature of the Left Fork, however, a hard and interesting ice-pitch must have been encountered. It is fairly certain that this fork will normally provide an exciting finish to the gully. In another ascent made in the winter of 1957, the ice-pitch required much skill and careful precautions, particularly in the region of the capstone. It was very severe.

CROWBERRY RIDGE   750 feet

Crowberry Ridge is directly under the summit of the Buachaille on the north-east face. Its upper half is a ridge inclined at an easy angle but the lower half is a steep buttress. It is bounded on the north-west by Crowberry Gully and on the south-east by the shallow Easy Gully. These gullies join below Crowberry Ridge where Curved Ridge down-curves to the north and joins the lower rocks of North Buttress. The converging waters go over a large waterslide below the junction. The waterslide is a well-known landmark in the approach, particularly from the west. (The Left Fork of Crowberry Gully and the right branch of Easy Gully join above Crowberry Ridge and Tower at the Crowberry Tower Gap.)

There are, of course, a number of approach routes, of which the most well-trodden, whether from west or east, is the one aiming for the waterslide and following the steep path to the left of and above it. This eventually slants up rightwards to the lower rocks of Curved Ridge, whence various obvious ways lead rightwards to Crowberry Ridge.

The routes on Crowberry Ridge will be grouped under three Faces and described from right to left in each group—North Face, North-East Face and South-East and East Face. Above the steep buttress part of the Ridge, about 300 feet high, all the principal routes unite on the 250-foot stretch of narrow, easy ridge leading, at 3000 feet, to Crowberry Tower. The Tower, at 3150 feet, tops the Ridge attractively, although offering no outstanding routes. It drops 40 feet vertically to Crowberry Tower Gap connecting with the brow of the mountain. An easy scramble of 235 feet leads to the summit.

CROWBERRY RIDGE, NORTH FACE

Between Crowberry Gully and the crest of the Ridge, are two huge, parallel ribs, separated by a long, shallow gully. The gully and the right-hand rib together form Shelf Route. The left-hand rib is Hyphen Rib, which is bounded on the left by another long, shallow gully called Naismith's Route. Diagram p. 46.

SHELF ROUTE   550 feet   DIFFICULT

Wilding and A. S. Pigott. September 1920.

The lowest section of Shelf Route is split by three chimneys. The leftmost chimney, starting hard against the wall of the Ridge, going straight up and then bearing left, is Naismith's Route. The middle and rightmost chimneys converge above the rib dividing them and are the normal and Direct starts respectively.

The normal start goes by the right wall and rib of the middle chimney. The Shelf in its upper part is loose and vegetatious and becomes a shallow trough, steepening to a scoop in the angle between the left wall and a small pinnacle on the right. At this point an upward left traverse can be made to the crest of the Ridge. The most direct route goes straight up to a square recess under the pinnacle and then by an awkward right traverse below it. A long groove then leads up to the level section of the Ridge below Crowberry Tower. Diagram p. 46.

Direct Start   VERY DIFFICULT

D. McKellar and P. Macfarlane. June 1933.

This is the rightmost of the three chimneys described. It is really little more direct. Three-quarters of the way up, transfer on to the left wall.

WINTER—W. M. Mackenzie and W. H. Murray. March 1937.

This ascent presented a very hard winter climb. The climb is seldom in condition early in the winter. (On the first ascent, the crux was the pinnacle section, which was very severe.) The right traverse might be very tricky; and the left traverse to the crest might be impossible owing to thin ice on the slabs. The upper groove might contain one or two ice-pitches.

HYPHEN RIB   300 feet   DIFFICULT

A. C. D. Small and J. R. Wood. September 1937.

Hyphen Rib stands between Shelf Route and Naismith's Route. Start in a bay below the chimney of Naismith's Route, i.e. the leftmost of the three chimneys near the start of Shelf Route. Climb the rib to the immediate right of that chimney. There is a stretch of easy ground above, followed by a succession of short walls, extensions of those on Naismith's Route. The best climbing overlooks Shelf Route. Diagram p. 46.

NAISMITH'S ROUTE 700 feet (to Crowberry Tower)
MODERATE

W. W. Naismith and W. Douglas. August 1896.

This was the original route up Crowberry Ridge, which was the name given to it by the pioneers. That name, however, has for long been given to the Direct Route and its variations, all next described.

Start at the leftmost of the three chimneys near the start of Shelf Route, that is, hard against the wall of Crowberry Ridge proper. Climb the chimney, which becomes a long, unclean, shallow gully with a succession of short pitches.

The upper part of the route leaves the North Face in favour of the crest of the ridge by an easy traverse on to a platform below the last two slab pitches. But the gully climb may be continued to join the final part of Hyphen Rib. Diagram p. 46.

WINTER—Naismith's Route is the quickest winter route up Crowberry Ridge. Times of ascent usually vary between two and four hours in proper winter conditions.

The best approach in winter is to start up the Direct Route and make a right traverse from Pinnacle Ledge (see Direct Route, north-east Face). In the upper section, the summer route on to the crest beneath the final slabs should be avoided. Continue up the gully until it ends on a wide sloping slab. Then comes the crux. From the top of the slab climb the short left wall, which overhangs, to the crest of the ridge, or else traverse on to the crest round a corner at the bottom of the slab.

CROWBERRY RIDGE, NORTH-EAST FACE

The normal approach to this Face is by the lower part of Curved Ridge and a traverse rightwards across Easy Gully to a well-marked moderate chimney of 20 feet at the corner formed by the Face and the Rannoch Wall. This leads to a terrace called the First Platform, where the climbing of the Ridge really begins.

Alternatively, scramble up to the First Platform from the lowest rocks directly below.

DIRECT ROUTE   750 feet   VERY DIFFICULT

G. D. Abraham, A. P. Abraham, J. W. Puttrell and E. A. Baker. May 1900.

This is the original Direct Route by the famous left traverse from Abraham's Ledge. Easier variations avoiding the traverse are described below. By the easiest line the Direct Route is moderate. Diagram p. 46.

Start at the right end of the First Platform near Crowberry Gully where a 45-foot pinnacle, not obvious, lies against the face (not to be confused with the 45-foot pillar lying against the face at Fracture Route some distance to the left). Climb a shallow chimney on the left side of the pinnacle to the Pinnacle Ledge at its top, from which a 15-foot wall leads to Abraham's Ledge.

Make an exposed left traverse and an upward balance-move on sloping holds, then go gradually rightwards and climb straight up on big holds to the Upper Ledge, which is 40 feet above Abraham's. (This Upper Ledge goes to the right on to the North Face and descends obliquely into Naismith's Route.)

From the Upper Ledge, traverse leftwards and upwards round a corner. The route is then obvious. The steep section ends with two long slab pitches (moderate). A stretch of easy slabs and a narrow ridge lead in 250

feet to the base of the Crowberry Tower (3000 feet).
Straight ahead, the Tower is climbed direct on its north
side without difficulty. Harder routes can be made on
the east wall (see p. 54). Its top is at 3150 feet. The
descent of the short side to the Crowberry Tower Gap is a
vertical 40 feet, but not difficult. The rock is loose on
all sides. There is an easy spiral descent from the top
by the west flank to reach the Crowberry Tower Gap.

From Crowberry Ridge, at the base of Crowberry
Tower, a pathway leads round the east flank into Easy
Gully and the descent is obvious to the top of Curved
Ridge. Use of this may save valuable time in winter.
Diagram p. 54.

Variations to avoid the left traverse from Abraham's Ledge

(*a*) PINNACLE LEDGE. *Easy.* From the top of the
pinnacle 15 feet below Abraham's Ledge, make a right
traverse on to the north face to Naismith's Route, and
return to the crest by the Upper Ledge. Diagram p. 46.

(*b*) NORTH CHIMNEY. *Easy.* From the right-hand end
of Abraham's Ledge descend a short chimney, join
Naismith's Route, and return to the crest by the Upper
Ledge. Diagram p. 46.

(*c*) GREIG'S LEDGE. *Difficult.* F. Greig, E. R. Beard
and R. Adamson. April 1907.

From the right-hand end of Abraham's Ledge, climb
a few feet up the north edge and make a right traverse
into an open corner. At the right-hand edge of the
farther wall is the start of Greig's Ledge. There is one
awkward move in traversing round the edge on to the
ledge, which then goes easily into Naismith's Route.
Return to the crest by the Upper Ledge. Diagram p. 46,

(*d*) SPEIRS' VARIATION. *Very Difficult.* W. B. Speirs.
R. R. Elton and G. R. Speirs. September 1938.

From the right-hand end of Abraham's Ledge, climb

up and round the north edge into the open corner at the start of Greig's Ledge; but instead of going round the awkward corner, climb straight up it to the Upper Ledge. Diagram p. 46.

THE CROWBERRY TOWER
150 feet

This Tower has an imposing appearance from certain angles and is a very useful landmark in misty conditions. From a climbing point of view it is disappointing, with much loose rock. Diagram p. 54.

NORTH SIDE. *Easy.* This is the usual line of approach from the Ridge. It is merely a scramble.

NORTH-EAST AND EAST SIDES. *From difficult to very difficult.* This face, which overlooks Easy Gully, is steep, exposed, and rather loose. It can be climbed almost anywhere.

SOUTH CHIMNEY. *Difficult.* J. H. Bell, J. Napier and G. Higginbotham. April 1898.

Climb this loose chimney which is an obvious route from Curved Ridge or Easy Gully.

SOUTH RIDGE. *Moderate.* The South Ridge is directly above (and bounds) the South Crowberry Tower Gap Gully.

WEST SIDE. *Moderate.* This is the short vertical side of 40 feet above the Tower gap.

FRACTURE ROUTE   225 feet   SEVERE

K. Copland and W. Smith. October 1946.

Above the First Platform, the approach to which is described on p. 51, the right half of the North-East Face projects well beyond the steep, reddish wall of the left half. Fracture Route is on the recessed left half and

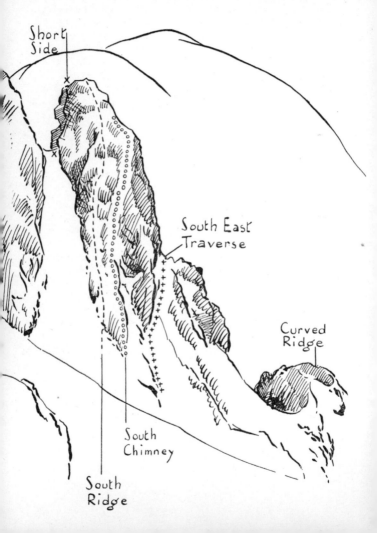

CROWBERRY TOWER FROM SOUTH

Short Side

South East Traverse

Curved Ridge

South Chimney

South Ridge

follows the line, first of a pillar lying against the wall and then of the V cracks up the vertical slabby rock above. The cracks later merge into slabs which, in turn, are cut by two deep grooves and the route finishes on the slabs of Crowberry Ridge.

Climb the easy 45-foot pillar. Belay. The left crack of the V is the line. Go up steeply for about 15 feet, passing an old piton, and then climb the more difficult and sustained section of 25 feet, involving two mantelshelves, to a good stance. Continue moderately above and finish right of the upper nose on Crowberry Ridge. A more difficult finish can be made by traversing left round a corner and climbing a crack left of the nose. Diagram p. 46.

ENGINEER'S CRACK   225 feet   VERY SEVERE

H. McInnes, C. Vigano and R. Hope. September 1951.

Start on Fracture Route and about 20 feet up traverse left about 15 feet to a small ledge in a thin crack. Climb this, using pitons, to gain a point where it is possible to traverse back right to Fracture Route, finishing on top of the first mantelshelf. Continue up Fracture Route. Diagram p. 46.

Direct Start. Very Severe. W. Smith. August 1951.

Climb the first 20 feet of the crack, starting about 15 feet left of Fracture Route. Diagram p. 46.

CROWBERRY RIDGE.   SOUTH-EAST AND
EAST FACE

This Face has, for long, been called Rannoch Wall. Because it is so well known for the variety and number of steep and interesting routes, which form a network over most of its area, its importance as a climbing ground is sometimes exaggerated. In the main, greater technical

No. 9
RANNOCH WALL

1 Chimney to Crowberry Ridge	11 Autumn Slab and Whortle-
2 Grooved Arête	berry Wall
3 Agag's Groove	12 Peasants' Passage
4 Curving Groove	13 Wappenshaw Wall
5 Juniper Groove	14 Shattered Wall
6 January Jigsaw	a High Level Traverse
7 Satan's Slit	b Girdle Traverse
8 Red Slab	H Haven
9 Route 1	○ variations
10 Overhanging Crack	

difficulty and exposure will be found, for example, on the West Face of North Buttress; and there is sounder rock on many parts of the mountain. None the less, Rannoch Wall provides great scope; it is climbable almost anywhere and does not lack steepness and exposure. The routes are described from right to left. Diagram p. 56.

GROOVED ARÊTE   220 feet to crest of Ridge
SEVERE

J. Cunningham and W. Smith. October 1946.

The route follows the edge formed by Rannoch Wall and the North-East Face, then veers right to join the last pitch of Fracture Route and the crest of Crowberry Ridge.

Start at a groove beside the edge and climb straight up on smallish holds. The well-marked groove on the left is Agag's Groove. It is customary to go left a few feet to take the belay in Agag's Groove at 90 feet. Thence climb on to the arête to the right and make a delicate right traverse on small holds into the groove. This trends right to the last pitch of Fracture Route and so to the Ridge. Diagram p. 56.

AGAG'S GROOVE   350 feet   VERY DIFFICULT

J. F. Hamilton, A. Anderson, A. C. D. Small. August 1936.

To the immediate left of the edge formed by Rannoch Wall and the North-East Face, a prominent groove curves upwards to undercut rock-leaves on the upper part of the wall. This is the line of the climb, which is the trade route for the vicinity and the most useful route of descent on the Wall.

Start at the corner of the wall beside a detached rect-angular block (just left of Grooved Arête).

Climb straight up for 90 feet to reach a block belay at the start of the groove. The crux is the short open corner a little below the block belay. Now follow the groove for 110 feet (moderate) to a large block belay. Continue up the groove until an easy left traverse can be made on to the open face beneath a vertical nose. Climb the nose and go up left to the sloping top of a block at 80 feet. Traverse left and go 70 feet up the face to the crest of the ridge. Diagram p. 56.

WINTER—H. McInnes and K. MacPhail; C. Bonington, J. Hammond and G. McIntosh. 8th February 1953.

The crux was the summer crux, namely the short open corner at about 80 feet. A piton was used for assurance. Difficulty was encountered in the long moderate section due to ice covering the holds. A second piton was used at the vertical nose above the large block belay for assurance. The standard was severe. The first party took 2¼ hours and the second party 4½ hours.

CURVING GROOVE   VERY SEVERE

150 feet to Agag's Groove. Length beyond depends on line chosen.

J. Cunningham and W. Smith. October 1946.

The start of the route is at the first small pinnacle left of the right-hand end of the Wall and about 20 feet left of and above the start of Agag's Groove. The first section up to Agag's Groove follows a not too obvious line between the latter on the right and Juniper Groove on the immediate left.

Go up a few feet until the angle suggests a leftward

trend to a position below some overhangs. Two parallel faults breach the overhangs and should not be confused with the deeper recess, close to the left, of Juniper Groove. Climb either fault on very small holds and reach a common stance and belay above. Continue directly above to reach Agag's Groove. A scratched arrow on the slab immediately above is just discernible. Climb the slab by a curving groove, thence left into a wide, very exposed groove, which leads to a comfortable triangular niche called The Haven. (See also Girdle Traverse p. 66 and High Level Traverse p. 66.)

From the Haven, the High Level Traverse or the Girdle Traverse may be followed—see pp. 66 and 67, and it will be seen that these in turn give access to other routes. The most elegant finish is to follow Girdle Traverse left and up to the pin belay below the overhanging crack of Satan's Slit, climbing the latter or the easier groove of January Jigsaw to the right. See pp. 60 and 61. Diagram p. 56.

JUNIPER GROOVE   150 feet   SEVERE

K. Copland and C. Lyon. October 1946.

About half-way along the grass ledge between Agag's Groove and a large semi-detached flake in Easy Gully there is a small pinnacle. Start 20 feet to the right of this pinnacle at a groove with a small, sloping slab near the foot.

Climb 60 feet up the groove, then traverse upwards and leftwards to a small ledge with a juniper bush. Step to the right round a corner, make an ascending traverse rightwards and continue straight up the groove to finish at the block belay below the nose pitch of Agag's Groove. Diagram p. 56.

JANUARY JIGSAW 250 feet VERY DIFFICULT

H. I. Ogilvy and Miss E. Speakman. January 1940

Start from the pinnacle on the grass ledge half-way between Agag's Groove and the large semi-detached flake in Easy Gully. The route follows the line of least resistance on this part of the face.

Climb straight up a crack for 25 feet. Go upwards to the left by large rock "stairs" to a big flake, and then horizontally right along a ledge to an obvious flake belay above the start of the climb.

Move right and climb by a flake and wall, then go straight up to the block belay below the nose pitch of Agag's Groove.

From the top of the block, traverse to the right round a corner into a slanting groove, which is the last part of High Level Traverse (see p. 66). Go up and right by the groove, passing the triangular niche of the Haven (see also Girdle Traverse p. 67 and High Level Traverse p. 66), and then gradually up left (by part of Girdle Traverse) to the pin belay below the overhanging crack of Satan's Slit.

Traverse upwards and rightwards, swing round a corner into a groove, and follow it for a few feet before working left on to a steep wall. From the top of the wall take the last 30 feet of Satan's Slit to the finish, or else an easier groove to the right. Diagram p. 56.

SATAN'S SLIT 260 feet SEVERE

H. I. Ogilvy and Miss E. Speakman. September 1939.

There is a large semi-detached flake in Easy Gully roughly mid-way between Agag's Groove at the right end of the Wall and a cave-pitch in the Gully below the start of Red Slab, well to the left.

Start in the easy chimney left of the flake. The route has a northward inclination and runs at an equal and opposite angle to that of Agag's, which it cuts below the crux. Climb the chimney, followed by steep, easy rock to some obvious flakes. Traverse left 20 feet, then go upwards to the right. Belay 100 feet straight above the start of the route.

Climb up for 20 feet on small holds, aiming slightly left, and then make a delicate traverse hard right for 40 feet. This ends in Agag's Groove 40 feet below the nose.

Climb 15 feet up Agag's Groove, break out right up a shallow scoop and go 30 feet to a pin belay below an overhanging crack. Climb the crack (the first 12 feet or so being the crux of the climb) for 30 feet and then easier rock for a further 30 feet to the Ridge. (If the crack is greasy, the best finish is to the right by the final pitch of January Jigsaw.) Diagram p. 56.

RED SLAB   270 feet   SEVERE

H. I. Ogilvy and Miss E. Speakman. September 1939.

Start just above the cave-pitch in Easy Gully at an overhanging groove.

Climb 30 feet up the groove, then an easier 40 feet to a small stance and belay at the bottom-left of a rock-nose. (At this point a variation may be made by climbing straight up a relatively simple groove to the height of the Girdle Traverse, and then with more difficulty up the wall above to the Ridge.)

Step to the right round the nose, traverse a ledge 20 feet to a juniper bush, and climb a red slab (piton above) on small holds. Make a right traverse round an overhang, and for a further 20 feet to a corner, where there is a piton "runner". The crux is the short vertical section above the corner giving access to easier rock and a belay.

Climb the last 100 feet of moderate rocks to finish on the ridge about 15 feet to the left of Agag's Groove. Diagram p. 56.

ROUTE 1   230 feet   VERY DIFFICULT

G. C. Williams, G. F. Todd, G. G. Macphee, I. G. Jack. June 1934.

Towards the left-hand or higher part of Rannoch Wall there is in its upper half a well-marked and vegetatious line of weakness, slanting leftwards and developing into an obvious groove. This groove is the final part of Route 1.

Start 50 feet above the cave-pitch in Easy Gully at a short chimney to the left of a rock-rib.

Climb the chimney to more open rocks and belay at 40 feet. Incline right over loose rock, then take a long slant up a narrow shelf, which ends at an awkward stance, where two sloping slabs are topped by a 15-foot wall.

Climb the wall, or make a short left traverse round a corner and so straight up. Finish by the long upper groove. Diagram p. 56.

OVERHANGING CRACK   120 feet   SEVERE

B. Nelstrop and J. E. Byrom. May 1940.

This route joins Route 1 just below the crux of the latter. Go to the start of Route 1 (see above) where a large red slab will be obvious on the left. Take the line of least resistance up the slab, beginning about 10-15 feet left of the initial chimney of Route 1. Climb to some spikes above the slab and very near the chimney. Belay at 80 feet. Traverse left into a dirty groove and go up to a 20-foot crack with an overhang at the top. Climb this and finish by a 20-foot wall above to join Route 1 below its crux. Diagram p. 56.

AUTUMN SLAB   80 feet   VERY SEVERE
J. Cunningham and W. Smith. October 1946.

This is a variation start of Overhanging Crack and is now Pitch 1 of Whortleberry Wall. At the top of the large red slab left of the initial chimney of Route 1, a narrow, sloping slab can be seen. The line of the route leads directly, trending slightly rightwards, to this small slab.

Start a few feet left of Overhanging Crack. Climb 35 feet, traverse 10 feet right and go over a rectangular bulge on small holds. Now go up right to a point immediately left of the small slab, which is the crux. Traverse it rightwards to a ledge and in 15 feet reach the belay on Overhanging Crack. Diagram p. 56.

WHORTLEBERRY WALL   390 feet   VERY SEVERE
J. Cunningham and W. Smith. 16th September 1956.

Climb Autumn Slab to the belay at 80 feet below the crux of Overhanging Crack. The next pitch has a run-out of 105 feet. Traverse horizontally left for 15 feet, then gradually upwards to a shallow groove, which is climbed to a small juniper ledge at 65 feet. Directly above are two thin cracks. Climb the left one for a few feet and transfer to the right one. Easier ground leads to a belay (on a stance of Peasants' Passage). Pitch 3 (85 feet) starts with a right horizontal traverse for a few feet, followed by a right upward traverse to a large grassy groove with an overhanging top. Ten feet below the overhang step right round a corner and cross the face rightwards to a small ledge and belay. The final pitch of 120 feet goes by a mossy crack directly above, then by easier ground to large blocks below the Crowberry Tower. Diagram p. 56.

PEASANTS' PASSAGE   230 feet   VERY SEVERE

W. Rowney and H. McInnes. July 1952.

Between the large red slab (common to Overhanging Crack, Autumn Slab and Whortleberry Wall) and the final pitch of Easy Gully to the left, is a shallow corner. Start at the corner, climb 15 feet and swing right on to a rib. Traverse slabs on right to a narrow rock ledge. Move along right to a stance and piton belay at 50 feet. Go up round a corner to a steep wall with a shallow crack. Climb to the left for a few feet, then follow easier broken rocks to the right to a stance and belay at 60 feet. Above the stance and slightly to the right is a steep corner. Climb it for 50 feet to a white rock spike. Swing on to a rib on the right, and continue to the top of the wall. Diagram p. 56.

WAPPENSHAW WALL   230 feet   VERY SEVERE

W. Smith and H. McInnes. July 1952.

Well left of the large red slab (common to Overhanging Crack, Autumn Slab and Whortleberry Wall) is the final pitch of Easy Gully. Start at the ledge above this pitch, where a steep corner rises. Climb up the corner, trending rightwards, until it is possible to move down right along an obvious traverse to a block belay and stance at 90 feet. The next pitch has a run-out of 110 feet. Move right under a big overhang to a rib. Move straight up under a smaller overhang. Go left for 5 feet past a detached block. Above are two steep grooves. Go up, using both grooves, and then move left on to a shelf. Where it broadens, follow an obvious fault up to the right to a belay. Go back to the left and up a short wall to finish. Diagram p. 56.

Direct Start   SEVERE

W. Smith and G. McIntosh. 5th June 1955.

This variation has the effect of adding a new pitch, because it goes for 85 feet to the ledge above the final pitch of Easy Gully at the start of the original route. Begin at the final pitch in Easy Gully and climb the right-angled corner there for 35 feet. Traverse right for 10 feet where a line of holds leads back into the corner. Climb to the ledge at the start of the original route. Diagram p. 56.

Variation to Pitch 2   VERY SEVERE

J. R. Marshall. July 1955.

This variation has the effect of straightening out the middle section of Wappenshaw Wall, that is, Pitch 2. From the top of the original Pitch 1 go up to and left of the big overhang and make a direct line obliquely right to the grooves near the top of Pitch 2. Diagram p. 56.

SHATTERED WALL   190 feet   VERY DIFFICULT

W. Smith and H. McInnes. 18th May 1952.

Start anywhere on the wall between the top of the final pitch in Easy Gully and Domino Chimney at the left end of Rannoch Wall. Aim for a point about 90 feet up, where there is a belay well left of a prominent deep groove. Traverse horizontally right into the groove and climb it until forced to move right round a corner to easier rocks and a belay at 100 feet. Diagram p. 56.

DOMINO CHIMNEY   160 feet   SEVERE

W. Smith, J. Cunningham, T. Paul. July 1948.

This insecure chimney runs up the extreme left-hand side of Rannoch Wall. Start 100 feet above the rock pitch in Easy Gully. Climb slabs for 100 feet to reach a wide chimney, then climb the chimney by its left-hand wall.

HIGH LEVEL TRAVERSE 80 feet VERY DIFFICULT

J. F. Hamilton. May 1937. Traverse to Haven.

A. C. D. Small and J. R. Wood. September 1937. Haven to Agag's Groove.

Approach from the Upper Ledge of the Direct Route, Crowberry Ridge, by a leftward rising traverse to a thread belay in the easy part of Fracture Route. Take a horizontal course across slabs to a ledge on the crest of the ridge, which is reached by a high step. Continue this line to a comfortable triangular niche, called The Haven. From The Haven descend a slanting groove into Agag's Groove. Diagram p. 56.

GIRDLE TRAVERSE   230 feet   VERY DIFFICULT

H. I. Ogilvy and R. Frere. June 1940.

A girdle traverse of the whole Crowberry Ridge may be made from Crowberry Gully, but only the Rannoch Wall section, from Fracture Route to Route 1, requires description.

Start from the easy upper part of Fracture Route and traverse 60 feet round the nose of the Crowberry Ridge into The Haven (see High Level Traverse).

Climb leftwards to the pin belay below the overhanging crack of Satan's Slit. Continue left to a wall opposite a projecting undercut block (the side of the nose that is the crux of Agag's). Cross this wall to make lodgment on the block. The sloping block belay above the crux of Agag's is then easily reached. 110 feet.

Traverse left, and slightly downwards, and continue below some dubious flakes to a belay at the top of Red Slab, whence easy scrambling leads to Route 1. There is no link between Route 1 and Domino Chimney. Diagram p. 56.

EASY GULLY   800 feet   EASY

G. T. Glover and R. G. Napier. April 1898.

Easy Gully is the shallow gully between Crowberry and Curved Ridges. One or two pitches near the top are not quite easy, but are easily avoided.

In winter the gully may be a walk and has often been glissaded, but there are sometimes two short icy pitches in the upper half. Diagram p. 4.

CURVED RIDGE   800 feet   EASY

G. B. Gibbs. July 1898.

Curved Ridge curves round the Rannoch Wall of the Crowberry Ridge. It begins at the 2100-foot contour and ends a little below the base of the Crowberry Tower. It is broad-based below and tapers towards the finish. It is the easiest rock-route on Buachaille and a convenient route of descent.

Start at the waterslide at the right-hand edge of its base. Near the start, and then half-way up, the ridge degenerates into an uphill walk. But after each easy section the rocks steepen and give most enjoyable scrambling. An easy scree gully leads from the top to Crowberry Tower Gap.

The route is recommended as a first introduction to rock-climbing. It goes through excellent rock-scenery. Diagram p. 4.

WINTER—In good conditions the Ridge can give a relatively difficult and attractive climb. An ice-pitch often forms near the base, although it is easily avoided. If snow-covered, the Ridge should not be used as a route of descent.

D GULLY   450 feet   DIFFICULT

I. H. Ogilvie. Summer 1935.

D Gully divides Curved Ridge and D Gully Buttress on its left.

There are four pitches followed by 200 feet of scree and grass.

In winter the gully is normally no more than a straightforward snow-slope. Diagram p. 4.

D GULLY BUTTRESS   500 feet   VERY DIFFICULT
          (by Direct route, otherwise Difficult)

A. Harrison, T. Addenbrooke, L. St. C. Bartholomew.
     July 1929.

The buttress is bounded on the right by D Gully and on the left by Central Buttress, with which it makes a right-angle. These two buttresses merge at the top.

Start at the lowest rocks below and well to the left of the waterslide under Curved Ridge. The 60-foot crux slab, about mid-way, is obvious from a distance and a useful landmark. Many parties find the indeterminate ground near the start of the Buttress a hindrance to route-finding and should look out for the slab.

Climb a slab, which can be avoided on the right.

After 150 feet of easy ground the ridge steepens and 80 feet of good scrambling leads to the crux.

The crux is a slab of 60 feet. The rock is superb and the holds slope out. A still more difficult route goes by the right flank. Alternatively, the pitch may be turned by a ledge and chimney on the left flank (easy).

Above the crux there is another 60-foot pitch on slabs. Climb on the extreme right-hand edge of the ridge. Thereafter the ridge becomes narrow and easy. Diagram p. 70.

WINTER—As a winter route, the Buttress can be a tough proposition, even if the crux slab be avoided. In the latter event, the right edge of the slabs above can be very difficult. In good conditions the climb, will certainly be worthwhile.

THE SOUTH-EAST FACE

The South-East Face comprises three buttresses and four gullies. These, from right to left, as viewed from a point a quarter of a mile south of Coupall Bridge in Glen Etive, are the Central Buttress, Waterslide Gully, Collie's Climb, Lady's Gully, The Chasm North Wall, The Chasm, and South Gully. Diagram p. 70.

Between Lady's Gully and The Chasm there is a quarter-mile belt of indefinite rock and heather, where many short crags, divided by broad ledges and shallow gullies, can provide both interesting exploration and much scrambling. Some of the crags are very hard and may be anything up to 150 feet.

Between The Chasm and South Gully there is a second belt of easier and more heathery ground, perhaps 300 yards broad. Beyond that there is no more rock-climbing on Stob Dearg of Buachaille.

No. 10

SOUTH-EAST FACE: CENTRAL BUTTRESS

1	Pegleg	9	Hangover
2	Waterslide Gully	10	Central Chimney
3	Direct Route c.b.	c.c.	Collie's Climb
3a	Variation Finish	d.g.b.	D. Gully Buttress
4	Kinloss Corner	c.r.	Curved Ridge
5	North Face Route	r.w.	Rannoch Wall
6	Spillikin	n.b.	North Buttress
7	Waterslide Wall	h.l.	Heather Ledge
8	Slanting Ledge		

CENTRAL BUTTRESS

Central Buttress is the face of rock, nearly 600 feet high, facing south-east, which lies in a line directly underneath the summit with Crowberry Tower and the top of Curved Ridge. Diagram p. 70. It has a distinct but narrow face to the north, the upper part of which is disfigured by a large white scar. This is an obvious landmark. In the upper part of the angle formed by the north face and the flank of D Gully Buttress is a succession of chimneys, and in the lower part there is a heathery gully, which bends to the left and cuts across Central Buttress to form a conspicuous Heather Ledge about 320 feet above the base. On the left the buttress is bounded by the very shallow Waterslide Gully, which is well-marked beneath Heather Ledge by whitish, pale yellow and black streaks.

The lowest rocks are about the 1750-foot contour. From the final rocks there is an easy traverse to the foot of Crowberry Ridge, so that more than 1200 feet of rock-climbing may be had with little effort.

ORIGINAL ROUTE   400 feet   EASY

J. H. Bell, G. Higginbotham and J. Napier. April 1898.

Start in the heather gully in the angle between Central Buttress and D Gully Buttress. Climb a tongue of loose rock and heather to Heather Ledge. Traverse the ledge leftwards to Waterslide Gully, where an easy crossing will be found. Follow the line of the gully, avoiding difficulties by easy rock and heather on the left. This is a vegetatious and uninteresting way of evading the Buttress. Diagram p. 70.

NORTH FACE   500 feet   VERY DIFFICULT

First 350 feet: J. H. B. Bell and A. Harrison. July 1929.

Last 150 feet added by D. Scott, J. C. Henderson, A. M.
    MacAlpine and W. H. Murray. September 1936.

The route offers a great variety of climbing by walls,
cracks, corners, chimneys, slabs, and traverses. There
is no outstanding difficulty on the section below Heather
Ledge. The rock is very good.

Start at the first convenient point to the right of the
north-east edge.

Climb a series of steep, rough walls. Near the top is a
short, steep and exposed crack with a perfect handhold.
Easy scrambling leads to Heather Ledge at the extreme
right of the south-east face.

While approaching Heather Ledge one will see the
large white scar on the north face above, with a little
recess underneath it. The route goes into this recess by
a traverse round the two pillars, which bound the north-
east edge of the buttress. From Heather Ledge, go up a
few feet to the rightward traverse, which is obvious and
well-marked. Go round the corner on to the north face
and so up to the recess. Belay. Descend rightwards to a
ledge and climb 10 feet up a very difficult wall to a ledge
slanting right. Follow the ledge to the foot of a 70-foot
chimney. Climb the chimney, involving a very difficult
step about half-way up, and reach a grass platform.

Above the platform, the route can be continued by
climbing the chimney and the final rocks above to the
summit of the buttress.

Much better climbing is had by traversing hard left
from the platform on sloping holds to a short, steep crack
near the north-east edge. Follow the edge to the top.
This is an exposed and interesting finish on splendid
rock. Diagram p. 70.

WINTER—R. Marshall and J. Stenhouse. January 1958.

On this ascent there was much powder snow and ice. Difficulties were found on every pitch. From the recess on the north face a right traverse was made beyond the 10-foot wall to the short, open corner, which was easier. The left traverse at the finish of the route was taken. The time taken was 7 hours and the standard very severe.

THE NORTH-EAST CRACK   100 feet   SEVERE

R. G. Donaldson, P. E. Burt, J. E. Spence. Summer 1942.

A variation of the North Face route.

The North-East Crack cuts out the right traverse from Heather Ledge by means of a long crack on the left side of the corner-pillar. It rejoins the North Face route above the white scar and just before the sloping left traverse.

Start 30 feet from the right-hand edge of Heather Ledge.

Climb 15 feet up the wall, then make a severe right traverse on small holds into the crack, the lower part of which is thus avoided. Follow the crack (delicate exit —severe) until easy but loose rocks lead to a well-defined ledge by which one regains the North Face route. Here make the left traverse followed by the short steep crack.

KINLOSS CORNER   350 feet   SEVERE

D. D. Stewart and A. W. Hay. May 1954.

This route follows a line of square-cut open corners near the left edge of the north face of the buttress. It finishes on Heather Ledge.

The start is an open corner very near the start of North Face Route but below it to the left. Pitch 2 is well-scratched and frequently mistaken for the start of

the North Face Route. It is a short but severe open
corner with an easy angle slab below. The next corner,
bordered by two steep ribs, is rather vegetatious.

Continue on the line of corners and turn the last one,
which is very steep, on the right, thereafter scrambling
to Heather Ledge.

At Pitch 3 it is possible to climb to Heather Ledge by
the line of either the left or right rib. Both have been
climbed but the left rib is preferable, since the right rib
too soon merges with North Face Route. The climbing
is severe. Diagram p. 70.

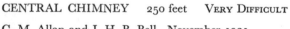

CENTRAL CHIMNEY   250 feet   VERY DIFFICULT

C. M. Allan and J. H. B. Bell. November 1931.

High Corner (Alternative Start, Difficult): P. D. Baird
        and R. N. Traquair. 1932.

Above Heather Ledge the right-hand half of the
buttress is set back from the left, so that a central rib or
corner is formed, just to the right of a marked step-up in
Heather Ledge.

Start on the left side of the central rib and climb to a
steep nose about 25 feet up on the edge. Traverse hard
right across a slab to a second slab on the right-hand side
of the rib. A steep groove, in its upper section a chimney,
rises above. Thread belay in corner above slab.

Climb up the line of the groove, first by two corners
to the right of it, then by a leftward move into the
chimney. Pass a projecting chock-stone. Beyond, the
chimney is easier.

Variations. Between the central rib and the north-east
edge are two prominent inset corners, which make alternative starts to Central Chimney.

(1) HIGH CORNER. The left-hand corner is 70 feet high and difficult.

(2) LOW CORNER. The right-hand corner is the start of the Gangway climb. It is 60 feet high and difficult, more so than High Corner. Climb a crack and then go leftwards along a grass ledge.

Both routes converge on the Central Chimney at the thread belay corner. Diagram p. 70.

THE GANGWAY   120 feet   SEVERE

J. Poole and F. R. Brooke. August 1946.

This route is a good double variation connecting the middle part of Central Chimney with the last pitch of the North Face route.

Start at Low Corner (described under Central Chimney), which is some 50 feet from the right-hand edge of the buttress.

Climb 60 feet up the corner-crack and traverse left to the thread belay corner under the Central Chimney. Climb the difficult corner above the thread belay. A large sloping rock-shelf will then be seen above, leading to the right. This is the Gangway, and the object is to get on to it.

Climb up the wall above, as far as possible, then make a traverse to the right and descend on to the shelf. Traverse the shelf to a big spike at its far end. From there, either go up 12 feet of steep and exposed rock, or else continue to traverse northwards at a lower level; both routes lead on to the final slabs of North Face Route. Diagram p. 70.

HANGOVER   200 feet   SEVERE

J. R. Marshall and A. H. Hendry. 9th September 1956.

Start at the highest point of Heather Ledge, a few feet

G

to the left of the central rib, where a heathery ledge (Slanting Ledge described below) runs diagonally up to the left.

From the foot of Slanting Ledge a crack springs up vertically. Climb it for 40 feet to a ledge, immediately above which is a thin crack cutting the overhang. Go up right and then left, passing a jammed spike, and climb the overhang. Then traverse right for 20 feet to a wide crack and continue to the top. Diagram p. 70.

SLANTING LEDGE   200 feet   VERY DIFFICULT

W. M. Mackenzie, J. K. W. Dunn and J. Ewart. May 1937.

Start at the highest point of Heather Ledge, a few feet to the left of the central rib, where a heathery shelf runs diagonally up to the left. Traverse the shelf and from its top end climb up until the angle enforces a right traverse across steep, exposed and sound rock. Turn up at the first opportunity. The upper part of the route is more broken.

An alternative start can be made by climbing the steep slab beneath the top left-hand end of the slanting ledge. Diagram p. 70.

SPILLIKIN ROUTE   200 feet   SEVERE

C. M. Allan, J. H. B. Bell, Miss M. B. Stewart. July 1934.

Start at the south end of Heather Ledge. Go 80 feet up a broad tier of easy rock to a second heather ledge, above which the cliff beetles. The following and final wall is the crux, in two pitches of 50 and 15 feet.

Start the second tier 5 yards to the right of the highest point of the ledge and directly underneath a short, vegetatious chimney on the top section of the wall. Go obliquely left for 35 feet into a steep recess; continue straight up on pull-ups to an edge below an overhang; traverse hard right and pull up rightwards on to a small niche with a good belay, 50 feet above the start of the pitch.

Slightly to the right above the niche is the short, vegetatious chimney. It can be climbed, but is not recommended. Instead, finish by the wall to the left— much more pleasant and open. In 15 feet easy ground follows and a belay can be found beyond. Scrambling leads to the top of the buttress. Diagram p. 70.

WATERSLIDE WALL   200 feet   SEVERE

W. H. Murray, R. V. Waterhouse, H. Cameron. October 1946.

Start at the south end of Heather Ledge. Go 80 feet up a broad tier of easy rock to a second heather ledge. The following wall of 60 feet is the crux.

Start the second tier 2 yards to the right of the highest point of the ledge (i.e., 3 yards to the left of Spillikin Route). Go 10 feet up a slab on small holds, then traverse obliquely leftwards round the corner to the face overlooking the "waterslide". Climb steep, exposed rock, including a mantelshelf, to a small stance with a good belay. Quite an amount of variation is possible on this pitch.

Continue either by a difficult corner straight above, or else make a traverse to the right on to moderate rocks. Diagram p. 70.

DIRECT ROUTE   320 feet to Heather Ledge
Very Difficult

C. M. Allan and J. H. B. Bell. November 1931.

This route does not continue beyond Heather Ledge. The rock is friable. Approach by a traverse from right to left under the lowest rocks of Central Buttress to a large, solitary rowan-tree growing in the dried-up bed of a stream coming from Waterslide Gully. A rotting tree-stump is alongside it.

Start directly opposite the rowan-tree.

Climb 190 feet up loose rocks to a small pinnacle, which sticks out from the face. This is a useful landmark, since the route is not easily found. Turn the pinnacle on the right or left and climb 60 feet to a grass ledge, where there is a choice of routes:

(a) Chimney Route. Follow the ledge upwards and rightwards to a vertical chimney of 20 feet. Climb the chimney and then 40 feet to Heather Ledge. The natural continuation above Heather Ledge is either by Central Chimney or Slanting Ledge.

(b) Face Route. Make a very short traverse to the left and go straight up exceedingly steep rocks to the southern end of Heather Ledge. The natural continuation above Heather Ledge is then by Waterslide Wall or Spillikin Route. Diagram p. 70.

WATERSLIDE GULLY   250 feet   Severe

D. D. Stewart and C. M. G. Smith. 6th October 1951.

Waterslide Gully lies immediately left of Central Buttress, separating the latter from Collie's Route. It is that part of it starting from the scree left of the Direct Route, Central Buttress, and finishing about the level of Heather Ledge (where the Original Route, Central

Buttress, concludes on the easiest ground), which affords
a climb.

The Gully is well-marked below Heather Ledge by
white, yellow and black streaks. There is also much red,
slabby rock on the actual line of the waterslide. Start
from the scree not far left of the large, solitary rowan-tree
in the dried-up bed of the gully stream. Climb the steep,
red slabs. At about 100 feet it is necessary to make a
delicate leftward traverse from an increasingly difficult
corner. Continue to the left extremity of Heather Ledge
by the line of least resistance. Dry conditions are desirable. Diagram p. 70.

PEGLEG   270 feet   VERY SEVERE

J. R. Marshall and G. J. Ritchie. September 1957.

Start approximately 100 feet left of the scree below
Waterslide Gully at the point where a distinctive, reddish
clean-cut rake leads up to a saddle on Collie's Route to
the left. Climb easy rock on the wall above for 30 feet
to a ledge and belay. Go up slightly right on steep,
water-worn rock and make an awkward mantelshelf on
to a ledge-hold. Traverse hard left (crux—a piton
runner was used here) to gain a ledge and piton belay
at 40 feet. Climb the steep groove above then traverse
right to a crack. Climb it to reach the top of a large
flake at 80 feet. Easier rocks lead to a steep crack, which
is climbed to finish the route. Diagram p. 70.

COLLIE'S CLIMB   1000 feet   MODERATE

N. Collie, G. A. Solly and J. Collier. March 1894.

Collie's Climb is immediately to the left of Central
Buttress across Waterslide Gully, and goes up the series
of short but steep buttresses which rise towards the

summit. This was the first route made on the cliffs of Buachaille Etive Mor.

Start at the lowest rocks and go straight up for 250 feet to a grass saddle underneath a sheer 80-foot face, which has been climbed (severe) but is not part of the original route.

Descend from the saddle northwards into Waterslide Gully, then rejoin the crest of the buttress above the 80-foot pitch. Continue straight up.

Below the saddle the rocks are good and almost continuous, and difficulties can be found; above, they are more indefinite and heathery. When this upper half of the route is under snow and ice the climbing may afford good sport and some route selection. Diagram p. 70.

LADY'S GULLY   800 feet   VERY DIFFICULT

Mr and Mrs G. D. Abraham. October 1900.

Lady's Gully bounds the left flank of Collie's Route and is the first gully to the left of Waterslide Gully. It contains about twelve pitches and forks after about 600 feet of climbing.

The climb begins when the watercourse suddenly steepens in long, deep chimneys of about difficult standard. Climb these, mainly on their south walls, for about 200 feet and walk over scree (escapes to right and left) to a wall of 150 feet, which forms a barrier. The watercourse comes down over the north end of the wall.

Start in the corner right of the watercourse and climb 70 feet by two steep chimneys, the second being very difficult. Step left across the chimney and round the corner and make a long, rising, leftward traverse across the watercourse wall to reach and climb a constricted 30-foot chimney. Easy rocks lead back to the gully bed.

The crux pitch is the 8o-foot very difficult corner above. Easy pitches then lead to the fork of the gully.

RIGHT FORK   MODERATE

W. M. Mackenzie and J. K. W. Dunn. November 1946.

This is the direct continuation and goes for 200 feet of mainly moderate rock ending at a cave, about level with the top of Central Buttress, which is easily reached to the right.

LEFT FORK   VERY DIFFICULT

D. Goldie, R. Goldie and J. Dunn. September 1954.

The difficulty here lies in one pitch of about 40 feet, beyond which there is only scrambling, unless a deviation be made to the South Tower. There is a cave formed by a huge boulder and this can be climbed by various lines, all of about difficult to very difficult standard.

WINTER—J. R. Marshall, I. D. Haig and G. J. Ritchie (finishing by Left Fork); L. S. Lovat and W. J. R. Greaves (finishing by Right Fork). 24th February 1957.

It is seldom that this Gully, or the lower section of it, is in true winter condition. The following were the conditions on the first ascent:

The first 90-foot pitch went by the summer route on the left wall, finishing by thick ice on the boulder at the top. The next section to the 150-foot wall gave no difficulty. The 150-foot wall went in two pitches, the first up the steep ice of the rib immediately left of the chimney and so up the crest to the left traverse across the wall to the 30-foot chimney. The traverse was icy and exposed, but the second pitch up the chimney, followed by a right traverse on insecure snow, was not difficult. In summer the crux is the next pitch and it provided a very steep and sustained climb on rock, snow and ice. The groove left of the overhanging section was used with a horizontal right traverse at the top. The last pitch before the junction gave 30 to 40 feet of near-vertical ice. There were no special difficulties above the junction by either fork. The time taken by both parties was about $4\frac{1}{2}$ hours and some pitches were severe.

SOUTH TOWER, LADY'S GULLY   250 feet
Very Difficult

I. G. Jack and C. R. Steven. August 1937.

The south flank of the left fork of Lady's Gully culminates in a high dome-shaped tower, cleft by a subsidiary shallow gully, which ends as a thin curved crack. This shallow gully is the line of the route.

Start from the bed of Lady's Gully and make a rising leftward traverse to a notch behind a rock-flake. About 150 feet higher a crowberry-covered ledge is reached, at which the route divides.

Finish the climb either by a crack and crazy arête to a platform, which is level with the top of Lady's Gully, or else by the above-mentioned curving crack to the top of the tower.

THE CHASM NORTH WALL 1200 feet Moderate

J. H. Bell, McGregor, J. Napier, R. G. Napier. December 1895.

The route goes up the rock walls which bound the Chasm on the north.

Climbing begins at about 1600 feet and the route

keeps to the rocks overlooking the Chasm. For the most part these are easy, but very difficult variations can be made. There are two especially steep buttresses, the topmost of which ends with a short level arête. The route is a good one for the "in-between season", when the rest of the mountain is in bad order with wet snow.

THE CHASM TO CROWBERRY TRAVERSE
1200 feet   EASY

G. T. Glover and Collinson. April 1898.

This is not truly a rock-climb but is a natural scrambling and trudging line, running up diagonally across the South-East Face of the mountain towards Crowberry Tower. The line can best be seen from Glen Etive and it starts at the edge of the Chasm below the first high wall of the North Wall, at about 1800 feet. It is not really continuous but is easy to follow.

THE CHASM   1420 feet

SEVERE (by South Wall Exit from Devil's Cauldron—
VERY SEVERE by Direct Route or South Chimney
Exit)

Of the gullies on the grand scale in the Glencoe region, the Chasm is the finest. It is the deep gully on the South East Face about a quarter of a mile south of Central Buttress, or approximately one mile by road south of Coupall Bridge in Glen Etive. It should not be confused with South Gully, which is a shorter one about 200 yards to the left.

Climbing starts about 20 minutes walk from the Glen Etive road, at a height of about 1220 feet. A characteristic of the climbing is that interest increases with progress and this is true also of the rock scenery; from a relatively open watercourse, the gully becomes a deep and impressive ravine flanked by high walls. Sunlight may be plentiful, particularly in the lower two-thirds, and there are a number of obvious escapes until entry is made into the Devil's Cauldron. There are sixteen pitches, excluding trivial ones, and, with few exceptions, the rock is clean and sound. The standard is mainly difficult to very difficult, but by the line of least resistance, involving the South Wall Exit, the standard is severe.

The gully is climbable in rain or wet conditions, when the best exit will be the South Wall or, perhaps, the South Chimney. The Direct Route from the Devil's Cauldron is very rarely dry and the route follows the watercourse. Most parties should allow between three and five hours for the whole climb.

Pitch 4 is roofed by a huge boulder. The best line is to climb the groove and crack between the boulder and the left wall—very difficult and interesting. Alternatives are to climb up the corner opposite on the right wall, which is wet and mossy with a rightward exit in spray, or to follow the unattractive line much further out on the grassy right wall.

Pitch 5 (at 1450 feet) is called the Red Slab and has a run-out of 90 feet on the south wall. A short way above, the gully forks. The left fork is a short tributary coming in from the south; the true gully is the right fork.

At this point, climb the exceptionally loose, yellow wall in the right fork. Alternatively, climb a safer, easier groove running up rightwards to the watercourse and at its top step round on to the bed of the gully.

At Pitch 8, called the Hundred Foot Pitch, the stream comes over a waterfall, 95 feet high. Climb the very difficult groove in the corner to the right of the waterfall.

Above the Hundred Foot Pitch, cross the watercourse

to the left wall and climb the "Piano Pitch" by a right traverse ending by a delicate move of very difficult standard on to a sloping chockstone.

At Pitch 10, called the Converging Walls, there is a cave-pitch of 60 feet with narrowing walls and, usually, a waterfall at the back. A little way out from the rear there is a ledge on the left wall. Climb to it and then straddle up facing the gully, until it is possible to cross over to the right wall by good handholds. Whereas this pitch is just severe in vibrams, it might well be very severe in nails and straddling may have to be replaced by back and foot work.

The Converging Walls may be by-passed by a pleasant ridge on the left.

Immediately above, one may get on to Lady's Pinnacle (H. Raeburn, Dr and Mrs Inglis Clark, June 1903 —reached from Pitch 12), which, after about 300 feet of rather inferior and heathery climbing, joins the slopes above by a little col. By a direct line this is, perhaps, difficult but avoids the Devil's Cauldron entirely and has little to recommend it.

Pitch 15 is the Devil's Cauldron. There are three routes:

(1) THE SOUTH CHIMNEY   100 feet   VERY SEVERE

N. E. Odell, R. F. Stobart and Mrs Odell. April 1920.

There is only one chimney on the south or left wall of the cauldron. Climb it. The first 30 feet are not difficult. The chimney then narrows and steepens till a platform is reached on the right. Open climbing for 10 feet still requires care and then broken ground follows. This is the most difficult of the three routes at the Cauldron but it is not an attractive finish.

(2) THE SOUTH WALL   100 feet   SEVERE

C. M. Allan, J. H. B. Bell and Miss V. Roy. June 1934.

Climb the South Chimney for 20 feet to a belay, beneath which make a very awkward move on to a ledge on the wall on the right. Traverse round the corner on to a broad ledge and take the line of least resistance above to the top.

(3) THE DIRECT ROUTE   130 feet   VERY SEVERE

J. G. Robinson and I. G. Jack. August 1931.

The grading of this finish is justified on account of the fact that in dry weather and even in relative drought conditions a stream of water, however slight, comes down the exact line of the route. It is exceptionally rare to find the pitches dry but in that event they will be severe.

Climb straight up the watercourse for about 60 feet to reach a small cave and belay. There is some severe, delicate work, often in spray, about 10–15 feet below the cave.

Now chimney well out from the cave and make for an obvious foothold on the right wall. A good pull-up hold is then within reach. The section from the cave to this point is the crux and is the wettest part of the Direct Route. Beyond are two small chock-stones, 10 feet apart. Back and foot work or straddling between them requires care as the rock is slabby. Above, the difficulties gradually diminish.

WINTER—The occurrence of true winter conditions throughout all or most of the Chasm is almost freakish. A few ascents have been made late in the season, when clear rock pitches have been reduced in length by snow banking; and even fewer ascents have been made when snowfall has been so heavy as to eliminate the character of the gully as a proper winter climb. No ascent has been made in true winter conditions, and February or March are more likely to present the opportunity. On such an ascent, time will be precious, but escapes are available.

SOUTH GULLY   500 feet   MODERATE

A. S. Pigott and Wilding. September 1920.

South Gully is the last and leftmost gully on the South-East Face, and lies 200 yards south of the Chasm.

There are eight pitches. The lower ones are easy and separated by long stretches of walking, but some may be varied to severe standard.

The gully lies 10 minutes walk from the road and offers an amusing off-day's scramble on clean rock.

STOB COIRE ALTRUIM
3065 feet

From the Glencoe Road, the summit rocks of the third peak (3065 feet) appear inviting, but the climbing is disappointing and its potentialities are negligible. The following winter ascent has been recorded.

CENTRE GULLY   300 feet

T. Graham Brown and J. G. Parish. 23rd February 1950.

This north-facing gully is the principal one on the cliff and is very obvious from a distance. At 200 feet the gully forks and the left fork was taken. Two short pitches of snow-ice were found.

STOB NA BROIGE

3120 feet

On the Glen Etive flank of this fourth top (3120 feet) of Buachaille there is a huge gully facing Alltchaoruinn, called the Dalness Chasm. This is several miles down Glen Etive from the Glencoe Road, but there are good camp sites and the area is attractive.

DALNESS CHASM   1200 feet

By Central Fork. VERY SEVERE. J. R. Marshall, A. H. Hendry, and D. Boston. L. S. Lovat and T. Weir. 21st August 1955.

By Left Fork. SEVERE. J. Cunningham and H. McInnes; S. Jagger and C. White. 2nd June 1951.

Dalness Chasm is more accurately described as a system of gullies. From the floor of the Glen it will be seen that the long lower stretch trifurcates eventually and the descriptions below are of the lower stretch followed by the central and left prongs of the trifurcation. The right prong has not been climbed. Once a party has penetrated well into this system, route-finding can be complicated, as tributaries are many and deep.

One may enter the gully after about a quarter of an hour's walk from the road. It is better to enter higher up, as some of the starting pitches are unpleasantly slimy. Drought conditions should precede an ascent, otherwise a wetting or even an impasse will result. There are few easy escapes.

Up to the first fork described below, there are a number of pitches, varying greatly in length. In reasonably dry conditions they will not exceed very difficult standard. One huge pitch, not many hundred feet from the start, could be more formidable depending on the volume of water. Still higher, the gully narrows remarkably and three almost consecutive pitches bear mention. The first is short but requires careful moving on a slippery slab to the left of the narrow watercourse. The second looks improbable and is very long. It follows a narrow rib to the left of the watercourse followed by a traverse into the bed of the gully above the waterfall. The third goes up a short, strenuous cave-pitch in the line of the watercourse.

After a long pitch, a junction is reached, where the first bifurcation occurs. This place is like an amphitheatre. (It can easily be reached by descent from the right or north bank.) At this point, the main Left and Right Forks branch off and it should be explained that the Central Fork springs up rightwards from the Left Fork, not far above this first bifurcation.

Records are now indistinct, but it is clear that the whole section up to the foot of the "Barrier Pitch" (Pitch 3 of the Central Fork) was climbed and explored frequently before the ascents of the Left and Central Forks. The parties climbing these Forks can claim no credit whatsoever for this work.

RIGHT FORK. This fork goes off rightwards in a great arc, curving back leftwards into the mountain higher up. A great deal of the upper section was climbed by a party rappelling into the gully and was less interesting than expected. The first few pitches appear very formidable and lengthy and are unclimbed.

CENTRAL FORK. To enter the Central Fork, which is the longest of the three, continue climbing up the Left Fork beyond the first bifurcation with the Right Fork. Below a small boulder-pitch, a rather insignificant corner leads off to the right to the foot of the Central Fork proper. (It is possible to reach the top of the small

boulder-pitch by a scrambling descent from the left or
south bank and this is what the party of the first ascent
did.) Scramble round the corner to the foot of a steep,
water-worn 60-foot pitch, which is severe. Straddle and
gain the left wall. The "Barrier" pitch (Pitch 3) is
immediately above. Climb the left wall by an obvious
cracked slab topped by an overhang. Above this, climb
a steep open corner and embark on its left wall at about
60 feet. Go up rightwards on vegetatious ground and
make to the right towards a small tree. Using the tree,
traverse right across a little wall and continue the traverse
for a few feet to the pool above the pitch, 100 feet above
the start. One piton was used and is in place at the
overhang. The pitch is very severe at both piton and
tree sections. Pitch 4 can be climbed on the left and
right walls, both severe, though the former is the more
difficult. A large number of pitches follow, of which
about ten are interesting. Three below the change in
the watercourse will bear mention: a wide chimney on
the left with a traverse on its right bounding rib (40 feet,
very difficult); a red left-wall pitch with a rightward
traverse below an overhang to the gully bed (30 feet,
severe); and a red left-wall pitch with a delicate leftward
traverse well up (30 feet, very difficult). Some distance
above, the gully widens greatly with a false grassy continuation on the left and the watercourse coming down
a large wall to the right. The true continuation of the
gully follows the watercourse to a shelf above the wall.
Follow it by a long chimney on the right (apparently
an off-shoot) to a moderate pitch above. Higher up,
beyond some easier pitches, the gully opens out on to the
face of the large right wall and it is possible to see right
down to the grassy trough. The water comes over a
cave, well above. Climb broken rocks to an exposed
line of good holds on distinctive grey rock, leading up

to a point left of and above the cave. The gully deteriorates after this pitch. Pitches become shorter, shallower and easier, and scrambling leads to the top.

LEFT FORK. The character of the Left Fork is different from the Central Fork. The pitches are fewer and longer on the whole and there is more walking between them. The gully is very deep and rather vegetatious. Regrettably, details were not recorded, but route-finding is not a problem. Three pitons were used on the third last pitch for security, as the rock is dangerously loose. This is the crux.

GRADED LIST OF ROCK CLIMBS

THIS list was prepared in consultation with a number of leading climbers, which is no reason for taking it too seriously. At best, it is an approximation, which may be of assistance; at worst, it should be an excellent source of argument or acrimony.

The grading is for vibram soles and the order of difficulty commences with the maximum at the top of each column. Every variation which is more difficult than the crux of the original route has been included.

VERY SEVERE	Diagram page	Text page
CARNIVORE, West Face, Creag a' Bhancair	—	3
SHIBBOLETH, West Face, North Buttress	24	26
NIGHTMARE TRAVERSE, West Face, North Buttress	24	30
PENDULUM, East Face, North Buttress	32, 34	35
BLOODY CRACK, West Face, North Buttress	24	30
GALLOWS ROUTE, East Face, North Buttress	32, 34	35
WHORTLEBERRY WALL, Rannoch Wall	56	63
MAINBRACE CRACK, East Face, North Buttress	32, 34	38
GARROTTE, East Face, North Buttress	34	36
WHITE WALL CRACK, East Face, North Buttress	32	37
DWINDLE WALL, West Face, Creag na Tulaich	—	6
BLUDGER'S ROUTE DIRECT FINISH, West Face, North Buttress	24	28
BLUDGER'S ROUTE, West Face, North Buttress	24	27

Notes:

BOGTROTTER, East Face, North Buttress (diagram p. 32, text p. 38) is not included in this list, because it is climbed almost completely by artificial technique.

THE CHASM TO CROWBERRY TRAVERSE, EASY GULLY and GREAT GULLY are not included because they are not, in any real sense, rock climbs.

FIRST AID AND RESCUE SERVICE

FIRST AID POSTS

AT the east end of Glencoe, there is first aid equipment in the house at Alltnafeidh (see map p. 2) and the key may be obtained there for Lagangarbh Cottage, where there is a stretcher. There is a public telephone box at the Glencoe-Glen Etive crossroads, and there is a telephone in Kingshouse Hotel (Kingshouse 259).

At the west end of Glencoe, there is a stretcher with first aid equipment in Clachaig Hotel (Ballachulish 252).

Rescue service arrangements are at present undergoing revision. Details at any given time should be available in Lagangarbh Cottage, Clachaig Hotel and the S.Y.H.A. Hostel near the latter. The nearest hospital is Belford Hospital, Fort William.